Studying Using the Web

Everyone uses the internet in their school work – but if you aren't careful you can end up plodding around the information fast track. It's time to change up to something more powerful. Knowing how to get the best out of the web doesn't just make it easier and quicker to find the right information. It can also transform your school or college work into something original and outstanding.

Anyone can type a few keywords into a search engine. But that's only the beginning. With *Studying Using the Web* you can find the right material, check its authenticity, transform it into your own original work and keep up to date on essential topics.

There are plenty of guidebooks that will point your way to interesting websites. They're great, but they get out of date very quickly, and they won't help you make something of what you find. *Studying Using the Web* is different. It's about how to find the right information, and how to make the most of it.

Studying Using the Web shows you how to:

- know what to look for
- make the best use of search facilities
- gather pictures, sounds and more
- make use of the human side of the internet
- learn how to test information with a trust CSI kit
- collect and structure your information effectively
- make text your own
- and keep up to date!

You could stay jogging round the information track. But think how much better you could do with the right technology and skills to harness a leading edge study machine. Move into the study fast track now!

Brian Clegg is an author and business creativity consultant.

Studying Using the Web

The student's guide to using the ultimate information resource

Brian Clegg

Routledge
Taylor & Francis Group

LONDON AND NEW YORK

First published 2006
by Routledge
2 Park Square, Milton Park, Abingdon, Oxon OX14 4RN

Simultaneously published in the USA and Canada
by Routledge
270 Madison Avenue, New York, NY 10016

Routledge is an imprint of the Taylor & Francis Group, an informa business

© 2006 Brian Clegg

Typeset in Garamond by
Keystroke, 28 High Street, Tettenhall, Wolverhampton
Printed and bound in Great Britain by
TJ International Ltd, Padstow, Cornwall

British Library Cataloguing in Publication Data
A catalogue record for this book is available from the British Library

Library of Congress Cataloging in Publication Data
A catalog record has been requested for this book

ISBN10: 0–415–40372–3 (hbk)
ISBN10: 0–415–40374–X (pbk)

ISBN13: 978–0–415–40372–6 (hbk)
ISBN13: 978–0–415–40374–0 (pbk)

To Chelsea and Rebecca for asking for help
with homework

Contents

Acknowledgements

Thanks to Philip Mudd, Tom Young and Kerry Maciak at Taylor & Francis for making writing this book fun.

The following items are reproduced with permission: screen shots of Google – reproduced with the permission of Google Inc.; painting of John Adams by Eliphalet Frazer Andrews, from the U.S. Senate Collection, reproduced with permission; screen shot of Mind Manager – reproduced with the permission of MindJet Ltd; text from the Church Music website www.cul.co.uk/music reproduced with permission of Creativity Unleashed Ltd; extract from Superluminal Signaling by Photonic Tunneling reproduced by permission of the author.

Chapter 1

Venturing out

This first chapter is mostly background for those who like to read around a subject. If you prefer to plunge in and get started, you can skip straight to chapter 2 when you've read the next few paragraphs. (Keep going for now – I'll let you know when to make the jump.)

First, let's get some basics about the book itself out of the way.

To avoid confusion, where I show words I want you to type into a web page I will make these bold. So please type **this phrase**, means type the words "this phrase" without those double blips (quotation marks or inverted commas). If I want you to put some text in double blips, then the blips will be in bold too – that way it becomes obvious if I want you to key in **this phrase** or **"this phrase"**. That's important because the two have different meanings to a search engine.

Each of the chapters ahead will improve your skills on making use of the web. You don't have to read them in any particular order, but the way I've written them made sense to me, so why not go with it? If you're determined to pick something up without waiting, I'd suggest checking out chapter 8 (making the text your own). The biggest complaint everyone has about students using the web is that all too often they just cut a piece of text out of a website and paste it into their work. It's little more than stealing, and most teachers and lecturers can spot it.

If you take this idiot cut and paste approach, your results will suffer. So turning what you find on the web into your own work is an essential. But then so is knowing who to trust (chapter 6) . . . and a whole lot more. So why not take the time to work through? It won't take too long, I promise.

Okay, this is the point to jump to chapter 2 if you don't want some background on the internet and the web. But it is useful to know a bit about your vehicle before you jump in and try to drive it.

Where did it come from?

Once upon a time there was no internet.

Aside – "internet" and "web"

You may notice (even if you don't care much) that I use two words that are often given capital letters – the internet and the web – in lower case. There's a reason for this. As a technology becomes part of everyday life it tends to lose its capital letters to show it's everywhere. It's just not special any more. We don't write about "the Telephone" or describe someone as "watching the Television." I believe the internet, and the web, have now earned that same generic status and deserve to lose their capital letters.

No, really – there was a time when the internet just didn't exist. And it wasn't so long ago, either. It was only in the late 1990s that the internet changed from being a special place for academics, techies and the military to something ordinary everyday people would take for granted.

Consider this. When Microsoft introduced its first half-decent PC operating system, Windows 95, it started something called Microsoft Network at the same time. This wasn't an internet gateway site like what's now called MSN. Microsoft Network was a separate electronic network you dialed into using a phone and a modem (we didn't have broadband back then). It was a private way to connect your PC to a computer belonging to Microsoft. Bill Gates and friends wasted a lot of money on the Microsoft Network, something they wouldn't have done if it had been obvious at the time that the internet was going to be there for everyone. And if the big brains at Microsoft missed it, so did a whole lot of others.

At the time, all the big computer networks used by ordinary folk were private, so it's not entirely surprising Microsoft went down that route. America Online (AOL) and Compuserve, for instance, were both private networks. If you belonged to Compuserve, you dialed up a Compuserve phone number, logged onto a Compuserve computer, accessed information on the Compuserve network and sent emails to other people who were also on Compuserve (luckily, back then, practically everyone with an interest in the technology *was* on Compuserve).

It wasn't that the internet didn't exist – it just wasn't something anyone at home or school could get onto, as we take for granted now. It seemed like an obscure also-ran for computer science students and people who got excited about Unix (whatever that was) when compared to the sophisticated power of Compuserve, or the graphical ease and elegance of America Online.

The internet was built on the back of ARPAnet, an electronic link that was set up in the days before personal computers. Back then, most computers were controlled by little pieces of cardboard with holes in them – punched cards – but a few computers could be worked with terminals – these looked a bit like PCs, but were little more than electronic typewriters, or a combination of screen and keyboard with no processor or disks. Until the ARPAnet came along, if you wanted to use one of the big, room-filling computers of the time, you had to use a terminal that was directly wired into the computer. Sponsored by ARPA, the US Advanced Research Projects Agency, ARPAnet was a way for universities working on defense projects to switch their terminals from one computer to another, even if that computer was hundreds of miles away.

When the ARPAnet started in the late 1960s, there was no real idea of connecting computers together, just of being able to flip from one to another, as if your terminal were directly connected to that particular computer. But soon it was realized that if information could move from computer to terminal this way, then it could also travel from one computer to another. By the early 1970s, the idea of electronic mail had taken off and in 1980 the inspiration came of linking together the various networks that had by now been modeled on ARPAnet to connect them together with an inter-network – a collection of networks that was rapidly becoming worldwide and together would form the internet.

In a sense, not much happened for the next 15 years – amazing, when you think how quickly computer technology changes. The internet grew to connect together many universities and a handful of businesses, but it wasn't something the general public would have come across. When we reach 1995, and the launch of Microsoft Network, the internet had become more widely available, internet email was more common, but the net was still largely used for connecting a dumb terminal to other computers, or for moving files from one place to another using a clumsy system called FTP (File Transfer Protocol).

What Microsoft hadn't spotted when they invested all that time and money in Microsoft Network was a burst of unusual internet activity at the CERN laboratory. CERN (Conseil Européen pour la Recherche Nucléaire) is a vast international research establishment working on high energy particles, usually described as being in Geneva but in fact straggling over (or, rather, under) the border between Switzerland and France. Apart from its leading role as a sinister location in Dan Brown's thriller *Angels and Demons*, CERN is a place where the basic components of the universe are battered together with immense energy in an attempt to analyze their makeup and understand their characteristics. And it was at CERN that the Word Wide Web was born.

In 1990, a scientist at CERN, Tim Berners-Lee, thought up a simple way to share information with others, not as an email or as an online discussion in a forum, but using something that worked more like publishing. Academics like Berners-Lee were used to sharing information by getting papers printed in journals, but this was slow and costly. Berners-Lee's idea was to make it easy to get a document quickly onto the internet so it could be read by other researchers anywhere in the world. Because there were to be no boundaries (rather than any clever foresight that the web would take off the way it did), Berners-Lee's little system was called the World Wide Web.

At the time, the publishing world had started to use electronic printing. Up to then, printers had to put bits of metal with letters on into a special frame to go into the printing press. (The letter blocks were held in two cases, one above the other. Capital letters were in the upper case, and small letters in the lower case, which is why we have upper and lower case.) With the new electronic devices, documents prepared for print included special instructions to the typesetting machine (big, clunky professional printers), called a markup language.

The markup language told the machine when to insert a new paragraph, or to change font or to print in bold. Unlike the hidden information that controls these settings in a word processor, the markup language was in plain English, distributed through the text, but with special markings that told the typesetting machine these were instructions, not stuff to actually print. Berners-Lee took the same approach with HTML, HyperText Markup Language, which instructed software how to display the documents on his World Wide Web. (If you aren't familiar with HTML, open a web page in a browser, then take a look at the source. Select *Source* or *Page Source* from the

View menu. All that stuff that isn't the text of the page – often in special brackets like this: <title> – is the markup language.)

By the second half of the 1990s the web was fairly easy to get onto, but there was not much to look at if you weren't in the research community. I can still remember the brief thrill of being able to connect up to a botanical garden site in Australia, and to know that those words I was reading were coming all the way from the other side of the world – but that was about it. It wasn't exactly life-changing, and there wasn't much an ordinary person wanted to look at. But with easier tools to put information on the web, the ability to use graphics and pictures in web documents, and the gradual realization by companies that the web was something they could use to make money, it took off like a rocket. In less than ten years the internet went from a technical oddity to a must-have facility that everyone would need access to, whether they were doing business, getting information for their schoolwork or just getting on with life.

What the web is . . . and isn't

You don't need to know anything about the technology behind the web or the internet to use it, but it is helpful to know what it is (and isn't) as far as being a study facility, if you really want to take charge of the web and get it to do what you want.

Let's start with what it's not. It's not a library. At least, as Spock might have said on the original *Star Trek*, it's a library, Jim, but not as we know it. (If you don't get this reference, do a web search on **it's life, Jim, but not as we know it**.) For a start, if the web were a library, it would be one where millions of books were thrown with great force through the windows each and every day to land randomly anywhere in the building. All the time, an army of spiders would be working its way around the library, cataloging what's in there and leaving cobweb links between the documents. And simultaneously a horde of virtual mice would be nibbling away, ceaselessly destroying information.

There are no librarians to decide what goes in this strange library. Anyone, anyone at all – professor, madman, enthusiast, salesman, crank, terrorist, president, even you – anyone can hurl whatever they like into the library. And at first glance there is no difference between those high-stacked volumes, no way to tell the good from the bad. (Luckily, as we shall find, there are actually plenty of clues if you know how to look for them.) A lot of the people who throw things into the library will be trying to sell something. As well as being the ultimate collection of reference information, it's like the biggest heap of junk mail order catalogs ever. Yet those salesmen may also provide genuinely useful information, to tempt you to visit their site. And there is no limit to the size of this virtual library. In principle it can just keep on growing and growing for ever.

Here's something else the web isn't. It's not comprehensive. It won't tell you everything you want to know. And it is never likely to. If you are looking for something that has been the subject of recent research in a university, chances are it's there. Pretty well any organization that is worth thinking about from the Nobel Prize people to the Academy of Motion Picture Arts and Sciences have a website (try www.nobelprize.org and www.oscars.org), as will any business worth dealing with. Yet there is a surprisingly large amount of useful information that isn't accessible online yet.

Take books. Wonderful though the internet is, much of the really good stuff is still only to be found in printed books (like this one). Wouldn't it be really convenient if all those books were on the internet? Surely it should be done as soon as possible. Well, yes, it would be convenient. But the trouble is, there wouldn't be any new books once the existing titles all became freely available, because the authors wouldn't be able to make a living. If the books aren't sold, but are given away to everyone on the web, the whole business of being an author will be destroyed.

This problem doesn't apply to old books which are out of copyright, and are increasingly available to access on online (more on these in chapter 3). And there are a number of attempts under way, most notably by Google, to scan vast numbers of books and make them available online in a restricted way. The idea is that you will be able to search for anything in the book and just get the small bit of text that sits around your search result. But many authors and publishers aren't happy with this, particularly those who write in small chunks anyway (like poets). As this book goes to print, legal disputes are underway between authors and the online scanners – the jury is out on what you will eventually be able to get to online.

Then there's the whole category of information that is either too obscure to have made it as far as the internet – no one has ever bothered to put up a web page about it, and probably never will – or that is too hard to get into the right format. (If you can't think of anything that can't be put online, try putting in the sensation of stroking a dog, or the smell of a fresh donut. It no doubt will one day be possible, but not yet.)

So the web isn't a library, and it's not comprehensive. Since many people have a fuzzy picture of it as a free library with everything in it, it's only fair that we knock out the third of those key words to totally shatter their illusions – it's not free either. At least, not all of it. The internet grew up in a time when freedom was a very important issue – and freedom of information perhaps most of all. One of the genuinely admirable boasts of fans of the internet and the web is that it's very difficult for any country (even the US, which still "owns" much of the hardware behind it) to control the net. It's a natural vehicle for free speech. But that doesn't mean you can get hold of whatever you like for nothing.

The majority of the information on the web is free, but occasionally you are going to have to reach into your virtual pocket for a payment if there's something you particularly need, and the owner is charging. Often this happens if you try to get your hands on the archive of a newspaper or magazine, or to get into some of the more powerful reference resources. Of course you can buy pretty much anything over the internet, but we are specifically looking for information. If you want to search back over the years at the *New York Times*, or to read an article that featured in *New Scientist* a few years ago, you no longer have to spend hours fighting a microfilm reader in a library – you can do it instantly on the web. But those nice publishers have a living to make too, and though they'll usually let you see a snippet of the information for free, if you want the whole thing you are going to have to either pay a flat fee, or a subscription to the publication.

It's quite possible, of course, that your school or university has already got such a subscription that you can make use of – ask at the library. (There's nothing librarians like better than being asked for help to access information – they didn't take that job just to be shelf stackers for books, or because they like using barcode scanners.) The same goes for huge reference resources like the mighty *Oxford English Dictionary* or *Groves*, the definitive musical dictionary. You can use both of these online to your heart's content – provided you have an appropriate subscription, and libraries often have them set up and ready to roll. They may even be able to give you an access code so you can get to these resources from your own computer.

So we're pretty sure now what the web isn't – let's also remind ourselves that the *internet* isn't just the web, there's plenty more to it. As we've seen, it was originally designed to make it possible to log into other computers remotely – and it can still be used for that – but when studying on the net, it's important not to forget the power of email and the information sharing pages that are variously called forums, news-groups, discussion groups or bulletin boards, depending where you look. There's more still – instant messaging, VoIP (Voice over Internet protocol) and all the rest – but email and forums will prove the most useful on our quest for knowledge.

Engage hyperdrive

Something that sits at the heart of the way we use the web, something that has become so commonplace that we don't really notice it any more, is hypertext. This is the idea of having part of a document that you can click on to jump immediately elsewhere, much as the fictional concept of hyperdrive jumps starships across the galaxy. The "else-where" you jump to can be in the same document, in a different page on the same site or on a web page the other side of the world.

Hypertext is one of those ideas that came along before the tech-nology to make it work. The word was made up by Ted Nelson, an ideas man in the early days of computing, whose books were a mix of original thinking and anarchic madness. What he wanted to do was to get away from the line by line march of words through a normal book, to be able to leap effortlessly from one place to another, checking a definition, surfing to related information, taking reading to a different dimension.

There was hypertext before the web – in the Windows help system, for example, and in a once-popular piece of Mac software called Hypercard – but it took the web to turn such linked documents into a multidimensional landscape of information that spanned the world. We might mostly forget that word "hypertext" these days – we're just clicking links – but it is lurking there all the time in that first part of a web address HTTP: that's HyperText Transfer Protocol.

To get moving, take a step back

You don't need any more context and history – let's get down to business. It's tempting to plunge straight online, but you'll get better results if you hold back a moment and think of exactly what is that you want.

Chapter 2

What to look for

The whole point of using the internet is that it's quick, right? Get to a search engine, type in what you need, pick up the result and you're done.

Well . . . no. Not always. Imagine you could see the whole of the web, billions of pages, stretched out in front of you, and you've got a question you want answered. You know that the answer is out there in that immense array of pages. But how are you going to get to it? You could jump in and flounder around – but you would do a lot better if you spent a few seconds thinking about asking the right question.

Important aside: knowing what you want and asking the right question are *not* the same thing. Take a fresh look at an old, old puzzle you may well have heard before. You are in a strange room with two doors. You know that if you go through the correct door you will be rewarded with riches beyond your wildest dreams. Go through the other door and you will die. Between the doors stand two men. One of these men always tells the truth. The other always lies. But you have no idea which is the liar and which is the truth teller. They know which door you should go through; you don't.

Now you certainly know what you *want*. It's to go through the door that will make you rich, not the door that will get you killed. But what's the right question to ask? Not the same thing at all. What question would you ask of one of the men?

If you haven't heard this puzzle before, make sure you think of a question to ask before you go on.

So what you want to know is which door to go through. What you have to *ask* one of the men (either will do) is, "Which door would the other man tell me is the safe choice?" Whichever door is pointed to, ignore it and go through the other one. If you happen to have asked the truth teller, then he will truthfully tell you that the liar would point you to the deadly door. If you asked the liar, he would mislead you by telling you the truth teller would point to the door of death. Either way, the door the man you ask suggests is the one to ignore.

It's just a puzzle, but it does make the point. Knowing what you want ("to write a 5000 word project on the link between use of fossil fuels and global warming" or "identify the main arguments for and against someone else having written Shakespeare's plays" or "create a newspaper from the age of enlightenment featuring two advertisements, two features, eight supporting articles, an interview and an editorial" – or whatever your brief happens to be) is not the same as knowing the right questions to ask a search engine.

Those have to be questions that produce the answers you need, and not too much else. Otherwise you're back to exactly the same problem as if you were just trying to look through the whole web, page by page, which could take some time. (If you can't imagine doing this, you will know you've finished when you reach this page http://www.shibumi.org/eoti.htm.)

Spot the computer

Let's imagine I've got an assignment to do that involves writing about the increasing power of computers. I'm a little on the lazy side, so I just type the most important word in the brief, **computer**, into Google. After all, using search engines well is all about choosing the right keywords.

These keywords are the essential words in a phrase or sentence. In English I might ask, "What are the essential developments in the increasing power of computers?" A lot of the words in that sentence don't do a lot. You can ignore all the little "the"s and "of"s and such – probably all that is essential is **increasing**, **power**, and **computers**, but I decided to keep things as simple as possible and stick with computer. (Note **computer**, not **computers**, because **computer** will pick up both.)

Here's the response I get from Google.

Google   Web Images Groups News Froogle **more »**
computer   [Search] Advanced Search Preferences

Web   Results **1 - 50** of about **1,630,000,000** for **computer**

That's not a fake. Google really was prepared to give me 1.6 billion places to look. If each one took me a minute to check out, I would get through them all in around 3,099 years without a break. (Just to show how the web has grown, I did the same exercise for a book I wrote back in 2001 and got a mere 66 million responses then.) But I can't realistically work through even a fraction of those results. There has to be a better way.

We'll go into getting the questions right in a more structured fashion in a moment, but let's just see if we can do a little better on that particular query. Even though the search engine came back with so many results, it does do its best to put them in a sensible order, listing the most useful entries first. Of course this is very crude – little more than guesswork – because Google doesn't know what I'm actually looking for, but it does use a clever system called page rankings to do its best.

These page rankings rely on a number of factors, but most importantly the pages that come higher up in the results will be the ones that are more frequently pointed to by other pages, especially when those referring pages are themselves important. So, for instance, a page will get a better ranking if a major site like the BBC or NASA points to it, than if a site advertising Aunt Maisie's Hairnets for Dogs has got a link to the page. That means the first 50 or so results are more likely to be interesting ones, provided you put in a suitable search query. Perhaps it would be a good idea, though, to be a bit more specific about what I wanted.

Putting **increasing power of computers** into Google came back with 18.2 million responses, but on taking a quick glance through the short summaries that appear in the Google results, I quickly got the idea that something called *Moore's Law* was an important factor here.

Doing a second search on **"moore's law"** took me down to 1.17 million responses, but more importantly, in the first four results I had an explanation of this idea from Intel, a very helpful entry in an online encyclopedia and a technical article on understanding the concept. We'll see more on this technique of modifying your search from what you get in the results, but the important thing here is that by asking the right question I managed to home in very quickly on the information I needed.

At this point, let's meet a few imaginary assignments. They are going to carry through the rest of the book, so it's helpful to get to know them a little at this stage. Each is in a different subject area; each has a different requirement.

- **The big project** – *Roger Bacon* Find out all you can about the thirteenth century natural philosopher and his work. Include a cover page and illustrations, and MLA formatted Works Cited.
- **The mystery** – *Stanford's bet* Leland Stanford, founder of Stanford University, once bet on a flying horse. Or did he? Explain.
- **The essay** – *Teleportation in fact and fiction* A 1,500 word essay, including diagrams, on fictional matter transmitters and real life quantum teleportation.
- **The quick summary** – *Composers of Elizabethan Church Music* Write a paragraph each on five Elizabethan church music composers.
- **The visual guide** – *Manet's locations* Pick three key Manet paintings and produce an illustrated guide for a tour of those locations.

Let's take each assignment and get together an initial idea of what to look for.

The big project

Brief: find out all you can about the thirteenth century natural philosopher Roger Bacon and his work. Include a cover page and illustrations, and MLA formatted Works Cited.

There's no real limit to this project. It's one of those horrible things, often assigned over a vacation, where the more you can get, the better you will do. Given the brief – the description of what we have to do – the first step before plunging into the search engines is to develop a plan of attack. This might change as you pull in more information, but it's a starting point, a series of key questions to ask.

Plan

- Start with a general search on **"roger bacon"**. Pick out references that seem to be about the right Roger.
- Having confirmed which country Roger was from, get some background information on that place in the thirteenth century.
- What is natural philosophy?
- What did Roger contribute to natural philosophy?
- What do we know about Roger, the man?
- Are there any pictures of Roger?
- Are there any pictures that fit with Roger's activity and era?

- What is an MLA formatted Works Cited and how do I produce one?
- Where can I read more about Roger?

Note the last of these questions. Something like this should be part of any major project. For a short piece of work it will usually be enough to get all your information from the web, but for a big project you need to pull in books as well. Use the web to get together a working bibliography – books that can tell you more about your topic. As you search for Roger, you will find mentions of different books. Some pages might even list books for further reading. Make a note of any books you come across. You won't necessarily read, or even look for, all these books, but it is a useful part of your information gathering. Later on you will find out a little more about these books, and decide which to read and how to get hold of them.

Not sure what that "MLA formatted Works Cited" is all about? We'll come back to it on page 140.

The mystery

Brief: Leland Stanford, founder of Stanford University, once bet on a flying horse. Or did he? Explain.

This is a deliberately obscure brief. The idea is, in part, to see how well you do at getting from such a fuzzy requirement to a result. Because the brief is so vague, only a limited plan is possible at this stage. Obviously we need to find out more about Leland Stanford, but what about this flying horse? We can only guess at this stage.

Plan

- Find out more on Leland Stanford. Perhaps try **"leland stanford" biography** as a search.
- Check the Stanford University website for clues.
- Background search on **"flying horse"**.
- The only flying horse I've heard of is the flying horse in Greek legends called Pegasus. Get some background on **pegasus**.
- Try combined searches on **leland stanford flying horse** and **leland stanford pegasus**.

That's about as far as we can go without finding out more. One of the essentials when planning is knowing when to stop. There is no point planning to huge detail when you don't have much idea where you are heading. Keep it outline.

The essay

Brief: write a 1,500 word essay, including diagrams, on fictional matter transmitters and real life quantum teleportation.

There are two clear strands here – the fictional side and the real science. Writing an essay, we want to make sure that what comes out is our own words, so initially we are looking for sources, keywords, and background to be able to build an outline of our essay, before filling in the detail.

Plan

- Get some background. Try **"matter transmitter" fiction** and **"quantum teleportation"** as initial searches.
- It may be that "matter transmitter" makes you think of *Star Trek* and the transporters that are used to beam up to the *Enterprise* – okay, let's also try **"star trek" transporter**.
- Look out on the real life side for references to science magazines and journals. They may be too technical, but could give you an overview, and will provide some key terms and names of researchers for further searches.
- Don't worry about diagrams at this stage. If you happen to spot something useful along the way, that's fine, grab a copy and store it, but it's best to get the words in place and then look for opportunities to illustrate.

Not much else we can do at this stage – we need those extra keywords to open up a subject that we don't know much about yet.

The quick summary

Brief: write a paragraph each on five Elizabethan church music composers.

We don't want to spend too long on this one. A direct attack seems best.

Plan

- Search on **elizabethan church music composers**.
- If necessary, expand the search. Find out when the Elizabethan period was. Search for composers in that period.
- Pick out five of the frequently occurring composers and search on each of their names (in double blips) **biography**.

If this hadn't been a quick summary exercise we could play around a little more with what we were looking for. It would be worth getting a bit of background on Elizabethan church music, for example. But sometimes you just want to be concise and get the job done – that's the point of this exercise.

Although this particular example is only looking for a summary, this is very similar to the type of web research you are likely to do for that popular assignment "produce a newspaper article/page/set of pages for a particular time or event." Again, the need is to get the basic facts in summary form to produce a series of short articles that might each be only 100 words long.

The visual guide

Brief: pick three key Manet paintings and produce an illustrated guide for a tour of the locations depicted in the paintings.

Do you already know anything about the painter Manet? That can be helpful, but don't rely too much on memory.

Plan

- Simple search on **manet** or **manet paintings**. Get some background information on Manet and his work.
- Identify a set of names of Manet paintings to do further searches.
- Presumably some paintings will be better than others in featuring obvious locations. Take a look at some of the paintings online to select some likely candidates.
- Pick out location names from the paintings, and also from the background information on Manet.
- I seem to remember Manet painted a lot at a garden in Giverny. Do a **manet garden giverny** search.

There is certainly no harm in making use of something you think you know about the subject of your research, as long as you are careful to really read the results. As long as I am half awake, I would notice that though **manet garden giverny** does produce a fair number of results (over 21,000 when I just tried it), the name that crops up again and again in the summaries is *Monet*, not *Manet*. I had got my impressionist painters in a twist.

Don't be put off, though. Making use of what you know is very effective, as long as you watch out for mistakes like this. For example, the **"star trek" transporter** search in the essay exercise was much more fruitful.

Simple rules for generating your search queries

This doesn't have to be complicated or take a long time. Often, when you go to find something on the web you can go straight to it (say, to use a street map site you've used before), or just type a quick query into a search engine and use the first response you get. But for anything more than this, it's useful to think a little before plunging in.

The process goes something like this:

- **Do I know which website to go to?** If so, go straight there.
- **Am I looking for a simple, single piece of information?** Try it straight in a search engine, or an online encyclopedia.
- **Do I know anything about the subject?** Think up an appropriate set of keywords that will home in on the topic.
- **Break down the requirement.** Look for different parts of the brief that will produce separate searches. Watch out for keywords that are best combined in double blips to make a phrase.
- **Is it about a person?** It's worth trying the person's name with the keyword *biography*.
- **Scan the first summary results.** Look out for patterns, repeated responses and keywords that will be useful for further searching.
- **Don't worry about discarding.** If a search leads you to a dead end, don't try to make something out of it, go back and start again. Be flexible and prepared to alter your keywords.

What to look for – essentials

At the end of each chapter, these "essentials" sections will give you a quick summary of what you have learned, both to help keep it in mind now and for easy reference later.

- It's fine to plunge straight in with a simple search . . .
- . . . but for a more complex requirement spend a moment planning your keywords and approach.
- Keywords distil your requirement down to a few, powerful words.
- Knowing what you want isn't the same as knowing what to ask.
- Take different approaches for different types of requirement.
- Scan your first summary results and look for patterns and repeated references to make new keywords.

Chapter 3

Smart searching

So, you've got a quick plan in place. Let's get searching. Where to start? With the search engine, where else?

Aside – search what?

We have become so used to search engines that you might not even have thought about the name. But why is such a nine-teenth century word as "engine" (think of "fire engine" or "steam engine") used for such a modern concept? As far as we can tell, the "engine" in search engine is a romantic reference back to the very early days of computing, when computers were sometimes called "computing engines". Back then, a computer was a person who did calculations, not a machine. The most famous early attempts at building a mechanical computer, designed but never completed by the Victorian Charles Babbage, were called "the difference engine" and "the analytical engine".

Guessing your way

It's just possible that before you plunge into the search engine, you might want to start with your imagination. If you know which website you are looking for, rather than making a general search, you may well be able to guess the address and go straight there by typing it into your browser. (I'm going to assume you are either using Internet Explorer or Firefox, but most browsers work in a similar way.)

Breaking it down

Web addresses consist of four separate parts. Take the popular site http://www.nasa.gov – there are four different bits in there, separated by some messy punctuation:

- **http://** – every web address begins with this (to distinguish them from other types of computer servers on the internet, such as the old File Transfer Protocol servers, which have addresses beginning ftp: Browsers will assume you mean http unless you say otherwise, so you can leave it off. The "//" bit just indicates that the first part of the address is a server (effectively a computer) rather than a folder or directory in which files are stored.

- **www.** – more wasted effort. No surprises that the www is for World Wide Web, and maybe 99 per cent of addresses follow up the http:// with www. But there are some addresses that don't start this way (for example the BBC's main site is www.bbc.co.uk, but its news site is news. bbc.co.uk), so your browser can't take the tedious typing away from you here. If you do miss the www off and it still looks like a web address – like news.bbc.co.uk – the browser will try that address. If it doesn't look like an address, Internet Explorer will do a search on it and return the full search results, while Firefox will take you straight to the first site that would come up in a search result.

- **nasa.** – at last, something useful. This is the actual address part which can be as simple as nasa, or as complex as a slogan from an advertising campaign (such as the intriguing www.ibarelyhavetimetopeeletalonediet.ca) – but there are no spaces allowed in the address. Those missing spaces are bad planning on the part of the designer of web addresses – there's no reason why the system couldn't have handled them – but it doesn't, and there's nothing we can do about it.

- **gov** – the bit at the end tells you a little about what kind of site you are visiting. In this case, the "gov" ending tells us it's a US government site. More on these endings later.

This is a pretty unforgiving way to write an address, but at least a URL (Uniform Resource Locator, also occasionally known as URI, Uniform Resource Identifier), as web addresses are technically called, is pretty easy to remember – certainly more so than the "real" internet address that lies behind the URL and looks something like 211.246.101.199

For that matter, a URL is usually easier to remember than a telephone number or street address. If you aren't convinced, the web address of the computer company IBM is www.ibm.com, the address of their headquarters is International Business Machines Corporation, New Orchard Road, Armonk, New York 10504, United States of America. The phone number is +1-914-499-1900.

Which is the easiest to remember? Can you remember any of the three? Chances are it's only the website address you can bring to mind.

Ending it all

The last part of a web address can have two components. The first identifies the type of site; the second tells you which country the owning organization is based in. Because the internet originated in the US, there is only one part for US addresses, but to make things more confusing you don't have to be based in the US to have a US address for your site – so many non-US companies have, for instance, a .com or .biz address. The most common endings are:

- .ac or .edu – academic (universities, colleges, etc.)
- .biz – company
- .co or .com – company
- .gov – government
- .mil – military
- .net – network company/service provider
- .org – other non-business organization
- .sch – school
- .tv – TV station

When a non-US country uses its country ending, this is usually tacked on after the type ending (if there are two options for the type, use the shorter one when followed by a country identifier, the longer version if there is no country code). For instance .com becomes .co.uk in the UK. Some of the more frequently seen ones are:

- .au – Australia
- .ca – Canada
- .de – Germany
- .fr – France
- .uk – United Kingdom

To confuse matters even more, many smaller countries don't bother with the .co (or whatever), and a whole extra set of endings are always under constant debate. For example, .ltd and .plc are already technically available, though infrequently used, because they're not likely to be guessed.

Once you understand the structure and endings of a web address, it's often possible to guess where to find a website without ever resorting to a search engine. If you want to come up with an address for a company, the first guess has to be the company name with .com at the end. That's easy with a single word company – it should be no surprise that you'd score a hit with www.sony.com or www.gap.com – but it's less obvious when the company has multiple names. Originally, companies fought the "no space" rule by throwing in hyphens, but no one was ever sure quite what to use, so most companies have now given in, running together the different parts of the name. With that in mind you can reasonably guess www.bergdorfgoodman.com or www.britishairways.com

It is also well worth checking out the company's initials – though www.generalmotors.com will reach their site, it's really www.gm.com Remember, too, if you are looking for a non-US company to try the .co.xx ending, where xx is the country code. You will find that combined with the use of initials in my own Creativity Unleashed Limited site, www.cul.co.uk It's also worth trying the .co.xx ending if you are looking for the local branch of a US company. So, for instance, you'll find there's a www.microsoft.co.uk (actually the address takes you to a specific part of www.microsoft.com). Don't forget there is also now the .biz ending to provide even more confusion, though these are still fairly uncommon because they are unlikely to be guessed.

Companies don't always get the name right. This can be because they've no choice as someone else has got there first and owns a site you would expect to belong to a more famous name, or because they unwisely go for a complex variation on the obvious name just for the fun of it. A few years ago, Alta Vista was the most famous search engine, but though its main site was altavista.com, they couldn't use altavista.co.uk, which belonged to a UK literary agency. They had to make do with an alternative until they bought up the name. Similarly, www.nobel.org doesn't belong to the Nobel Prize organization, www.whitehouse.com has nothing to do with the US president, and you'll find the publisher Simon & Schuster not at simonschuster.com or simonandschuster.com, but at the entirely impossible to guess www.simonsays.com

Not having an obvious match with the organization's name is significantly more common when looking for, for instance, a university site – while www.harvard.edu and www.ucla.edu are the right addresses to go for, some universities seem to delight in having a name that is hard to guess. So the University of Charleston, for example is www.uchaswv.edu and Cambridge University is www.cam.ac.uk (though if you type in www.cambridge.ac.uk you do get a page that helpfully tells you the correct address). Even so, it's worth taking a quick guess before asking for help.

Okay, you've done as much as you can flying solo. Now it really is time to hit the search engines.

Hitting the engines

Search Portfolio

We all tend to have a favorite search engine, but the results from different engines can be quite different, and it's useful to be prepared to look elsewhere too. The world's favorite search engine is Google, and it ought to be one of your options, but there is a wider range of possibilities here. If you live outside the US, look out for a local variant like www.google.co.uk, which will give you the option of only looking at pages from your country – this is particularly useful if you want to buy something.

- **Google** (www.google.com) Google is the best known of the search engines, and probably still the best of the bunch with an ever-expanding set of facilities, like the Google Earth satellite photograph program and Google Books.
- **Yahoo** (www.yahoo.com) Yahoo was originally a human edited directory of websites rather than a search engine. The directory is still there, but now there's a very powerful search engine too – Google's closest rival.
- **MSN Search** (search.msn.com) Microsoft's search page used to be a front for Yahoo, but MSN now has its own search engine, and includes access to the Encarta encyclopedia as part of the search.
- **Ask Jeeves** (www.askjeeves.com) Ask Jeeves came to fame for its "natural language" interface that seemed to understand real questions like "How many counties are there in Ireland?" Askjeeves has moved to be more of a conventional search engine, and remains a useful alternative to the three above.
- **Alta Vista** (www.altavista.com) Once the biggest name in search, Alta Vista lost its way and its position on top. Alta Vista now uses Yahoo's search engine, but gives you a different way of getting to it.

So you've chosen a search engine and you are ready to go. But before you use your entire assignment as your search term (the "search term" is the word, or phrase, you type in), think a moment about anything you can do to minimize the amount of junk you get back, and make it easier on yourself when it comes to finding the important stuff.

First trim out unnecessary words like "the" – the search engine will probably do this anyway, but it helps makes your search term more concise.

Then, look for words that you want grouped together. A good search engine will do the best it can from what you've typed, but the English language is very difficult for computers to understand.

Aside – getting a computer to understand English

If you think it should be easy for a computer to understand a normal English phrase – after all, you usually cope with it pretty well – imagine a computer trying to understand the phrase "fruit flies like an apple".

Are we talking about the sort of food that the insects called fruit flies like (an apple), or are we talking about the aerodynamics of fruit, suggesting that fruit, in general, flies the way an apple does? Who knows? Human readers can usually guess from the context (the surrounding text that hints at what the sentence means), but a search engine doesn't have that luxury.

People have been trying for many years to be able to get a computer to understand English, and the results are still pretty poor. If you would like to see how computers manage, try out the state of the art chatbot, www.jabberwacky.com This is a piece of software that tries to pretend it's a human being and have a conversation. Even though this program is one of the best around, you will very soon find that it says something stupid, making it clear that it hasn't really got a clue what you mean.

And that's just written English. It's even harder if the computer has to interpret the words you speak as well. Next time you see a humanoid robot in a story on TV, having an apparently normal conversation (never mind the complexity of just getting a robot to walk, or to look like a human), listen to the way it seems able to talk like a person and to understand what is said to it. Unless the TV show is set a long way into the future, they've got that wrong in a big way.

Double blips

You can help the computer understand what you want by careful use of the search engine's simplest and most powerful secret weapon, the double blips.

Say you wanted to find out if there was a connection between the author Henry James and the singer/actor Dean Martin. You might type **henry james dean martin** into a search engine. The trouble is, when I tried this I got a real mess of a response. Some of the results seemed to assume I wanted to know about the movie actor James Dean. Others just had (common enough) names like "Henry" and "Martin" scattered around the text with no connection to either of the people I had in mind.

If, however, I had put in my search as **"henry james" "dean martin"**, including those double blips, then I would only see articles that had both Henry James and Dean Martin in them, with each name as a complete unit. Putting double blips (also known as quotes, quotation marks or inverted commas) around a phrase such as **"elizabethan church music"** only returns results where all the words in the phrase appear together in that order.

Before you make your search, see if there are any combinations of words you definitely want together – the chances are you will greatly increase the accuracy of your hit rate by grouping them in double blips.

Hot tip – forget upper case

Don't bother with upper case when entering a search term. The search engine will either ignore it, or assume you *only* want items with the upper case lettering. Keep it simple. If you put in **oscar** it will find oscar, Oscar and OSCAR (in fact, even oscaR) without any problem.

Checking your options

Double blips are a great help, but they aren't all the engines have to offer. Search engines have plenty more tricks up their sleeves to make for a better result. Before we get smarter in our searching, though, let's make sure that we are getting the results in the most convenient way.

Most search engines have a preferences or options page (for Google, look just to the right of the box you type the search into for a little link labeled "Preferences"). Before you go any further with searching, explore the preferences and get the results the way you would like them best. You only need do this once on any particular computer – the search engine will store your preferences away.

In the case of Google there are two options that are useful, down at the bottom of the preferences page. First there's a setting showing number of results displayed on the page. This starts off at 10, which is fine if you have a slow dialup connection, but anyone with broadband or another form of quick connection can benefit from increasing this to (say) 50 results per page. It makes the initial loading of the page a little slower, but is more than repaid by not having to switch search results page so often.

The other useful facility is the option to open results pages in a new window. This probably won't suit you all the time – it's the sort of thing you might want to switch on and off – but if you are working through a good number of search results, it can be handy to keep the results in front of you and bring up each of the target pages in a separate window rather than having to keep switching back and forward between the two.

Special characters and going Boolean

Meanwhile, back at the search itself, let's throw in a few more special characters. Put + immediately in front of a word or phrase (no space between + and the word) and this forces Google to only display results containing that word. This used to be popular when search engines were less effective at putting the best results first. It meant you could identify those words in your search term that were absolutely essential. The + is rarely necessary any more, but can occasionally come in useful. That's because search engines tend to ignore common words like "and" or numbers. If you aren't sure whether something is being ignored, Google, for instance, will comment on any ignored words immediately under the search box at the top of the results screen.

If a word you really want to search for is being ignored, use + in front of it to force it to be part of the search. Google gives the example of using **Star Wars Episode +I** (that's the capital letter I – the Roman numeral 1, not the digit 1 – at the end of the search term) to search for Episode One of the *Star Wars* saga. It will give better results than **Star Wars Episode I**, which also finds, for example, *Star Wars Episode II*.

More valuable is the Boolean search, which brings in terms like **not** and the chance to scatter your search term with round brackets (like these). That **not** simply means I want results which *don't* include the word or phrase after the "not" keyword, while brackets link together combinations of words so the search engine knows what to do with them.

You need those brackets because computers are so literal – they need leading all the time. For example, let's say I started by using the search phrase **dogs and rabbits or guinea pigs but not cats** – I knew what I meant, but this is just too confusing for the poor search engine. Am I looking for a page that has information on dogs and also has information on either rabbits or guinea pigs, or am I looking for a page that has either facts about dogs and rabbits, or about guinea pigs on their own? Do I want to know about pigs, but not about cats?

I can make things clear by grouping words together, using brackets and the good old double blips. If I ask instead for **dogs and (rabbits or "guinea pigs") but not cats**, I am much more likely to get a good response. Putting "guinea pigs" in those double blips removes any confusion with the ordinary variety of pig, and different uses of the word "guinea", while the bracket around (rabbits or "guinea pigs") makes it clear that I'm looking for dogs, and I also want at least one of rabbits or guinea pigs – it doesn't matter which. That phrase would work in a search engine, but generally they will assume the "and" and the "but", so there's no need to include them. So the neatest form is **dogs (rabbits or "guinea pigs") not cats**

Aside – and and?

Did the repetition of "and" look a bit odd when you read about the "and" and the "but" in the previous paragraph? See if you can think of a sentence that has five "and"s in a row. Don't read on until you've tried.

A man was painting a sign for a store called Smith and Jones. After he's finished, he looks at it and sighs: "I've not left enough space between Smith and And and And and Jones."

It's even better if you read it aloud. In fact you could even stretch it to seven "and"s by cheating a little and coming up with particular names on the sign.

A man was painting a sign for a store called Brand and Andy. After he's finished, he looks at it and sighs: "I've not left enough space between Brand and And and And and Andy."

Nothing to do with searching the web, but fun.

So the compact way of putting our animal query into a search engine would be **dogs (rabbits or "guinea pigs") not cats** – or even **dogs (rabbits or "guinea pigs")** –cats as you can use a minus sign immediately in front of a word to say you don't want it to appear. This might look a little messy on the page of a book, where it's easy to confuse a minus sign and a dash or hyphen, but it is simple to type.

> **!   Hot tip – where to put the brackets**
>
> Not sure where to put your brackets? The trick is to read the innermost brackets first, turning what is in them to a single item in your mind, then work outwards. So, for instance, if I have the search **texas and (michigan or (florida and california))**, I start with the brackets that are inside other ones and lump together Florida and California. I then move out a level and see I need either both Florida and California, or Michigan. And finally, moving outside the last bracket, I am looking for Texas and either Michigan or both Florida and California!

Can't remember those commands? They will get familiar pretty quickly, but if in doubt, it's time to get advanced. If you can't remember the special words to use, click on the Advanced Search option. Here you can fill in just what you need, with separate boxes for words you want, phrases, words you don't want and so on.

Going to the next level

Most of the time you can get along just fine by sticking to your favorite search engine – but the different engines do return different results, thanks to the varied approaches they take to finding their way around the web.

Wouldn't it be useful if something could take your search requirement, push it out to a range of search engines, pull together the results and present the links on a single page? Well, yes, it would. And luckily something does. One of the best kept secrets of web searching is the existence of those little gems known as meta search engines.

Mind my meta search

Try out these meta search engines:

- **Dogpile** (www.dogpile.com) Dogpile is the best known of the meta search engines – simple and straightforward.
- **Metacrawler** (www.metacrawler.com) Metacrawler is a sister to Dogpile with the same approach but a different way of asking for your search.
- **Jux2** (www.jux2.com) Jux2 is more sophisticated than Dogpile, telling you what's in and is missing from different sources, but is not always so easy to use.

Since meta search engines give you the best of all worlds, you might wonder why you should ever use an ordinary search engine again? Meta search engines do tend to limit the result to a relatively small number of responses – so if you are looking for a wide range of information to check through, you would be better off going to one of the full scale search engines. And meta search can't cope with all the fiddly detail of a more complex search term. Even so, there is no doubt that a meta search will produce sources that a single search engine wouldn't.

A good way of approaching these engines is to try out Jux2 for a few searches. This will tell you just what you would have missed if you'd relied on the engine you normally go with – really helpful to get an idea of what benefit you are getting from meta search. If you find that using a meta search is really helping, try out Dogpile or Metacrawler too and consider making a meta search engine your first point of call.

A game of two halves

Using a search engine well doesn't stop at the point where you've come up with a sensible search query and assembled a collection of results. You have to make something of those results, and that's where the art of searching on the web really comes into its own. Here is what we might see as the first few results in response to our search for **elizabethan church music composers**:

Search on Elizabethan church music composers

Note that these are not real websites, just an idea of what you might get. The part of the result with the website name, cached link etc. that you would normally see in results has been omitted so we can concentrate on the parts that matter.

1   Greatest English **Composers** of **Elizabethan** Times
Many of the most famous **musical composers** lived in England during this time of flourishing **musical** development. The **Church** played a big role in the lives of . . .

2   **Elizabethan Church music** In Elizabethan England, the high vaults of late Gothic architecture echoed . . . and Byrd. the **church composers** of the period wrote **music** that was both passionate and . . .

3   John Dowland: **Elizabethan music composer** Dowland's **music** was universally popular in Elizabethan times (the pop of his day) . . . rarely involved in the **church** . . .

4   Renaissance **Music** (1450–1600) The **composers** marked with asterisks are the most important to know. Byrd, Tallis . . . **Church Music** The style of renaissance **church music** is described as choral polyphony . . .

5   Arts: **Music:** Composition: **Composers:** Eduard Lassen LASSEN, EDUARD (1830–1904), Belgian **musical composer,** . . . **Church music** was much less popular than secular. Instrumental music, which until recently was integrated . . .

6   BSCM: England through to 1635 Thematic Indexes of **Composers.** Latin and English **Church Music** 1525–1635: The **Composers** . . . Tudor and **Elizabethan** compositions by a range . . .

7   Christina Aguilera's Greatest Hits Hot **music** CDs, **church** and gospel, electronic to **Elizabethan,** greatest modern **music composers** . . .

> 8 **Church music – William Byrd** In case you were beginning to think that all there was to Byrd was the famous 3 masses and a couple of motets, this CD helpfully fleshes out one of the greatest of the Tudor and **Elizabethan church composers** . . .
>
> 9 OUR 57TH BOOK ON GREAT **MUSIC COMPOSERS** He has been responsible for much **church music**, but many of his orchestral . . . This remarkable book, 'British Light **Music Composers**' (ISBN 1873413 38 X) is currently . . .

Don't jump straight in to the first item you see, but check out the result for obvious telltale clues as to whether or not it's going to be useful. This only takes a second or two, but saves a lot of time plunging into unnecessary links. Look at the sample text that comes after the title of the page (for example in item 8 above, this begins "In case you were beginning . . .").

Does the sample text seem to be about the subject that you are looking for? Does it show sensible uses of the keywords in your search term? Remember, I'm looking for **elizabethan church music composers**. Because of this, I wouldn't bother with the John Dowland link above (number 3), because the word "church" isn't particularly linked to music – this may well not be a relevant site. Similarly, our link number 5 obviously had the right words somewhere, but is about a nineteenth century composer, while link 9 is about a book, and at that a book on "light music," which is hardly likely to be a useful site for what I want.

Look out for shops. It's inevitable that this search would pull up plenty of results that involve selling church music CDs. In some searches, that can still be quite useful. For instance, it's worth investigating the Byrd entry, number 8 above, even though it is selling CDs, because there seems to be some information too. But if the link is to a straightforward CD shop, rather than a specialist site, or to a site like eBay, there is rarely any point following it up (unless you actually want to buy a CD!).

Look out also for opportunist sites that load a page with lots of words that aren't particularly relevant. The Christina Aguilera result (number 7), for example, is highly unlikely to tell you a lot about Elizabethan composers.

With a bit of eye training, you will find it easy to home in on the sites that are most likely to come up with a valuable result. At first glance, in the list above, I would take a look at numbers 1, 2, 4, 6, and 8.

As you glance through the results, look out for common factors that seem likely to lead onto something more. William Byrd is mentioned several times, so it might be worth doing a secondary search on William Byrd (it's a great name, if no other reason), perhaps as **"william byrd" biography** – and similarly for a few other composers. Remember how doing a search on **increasing power of computers** quickly brought Moore's Law to my attention, which then itself became the subject of a search. Be prepared to spring off in a different direction when given an interesting lead like this.

> # ! Hot tip – where did it go?
>
> The web is a fast-changing place. A web page can be here today and gone tomorrow. Although search engines try to keep as up-to-date as possible, they can't check every page every minute, just to be sure that something that they have indexed is still there. So sometimes, when you click on a link, the page you've asked for won't exist.
>
> This could happen dramatically – giving an error message that tells you an address can't be found (the most popular is Error 404, which sounds frighteningly technical, but is just the HTTP server's way of saying "nope, can't find that") – or subtly, where a web page appears, but you can't see the information you wanted anywhere on the page.
>
> Often you won't be able to find what you wanted because the page in question is updated frequently – perhaps it's a weekly news page, and every week new information replaces the old, so the result you found on the search engine is a view into the past – a bit like staring into the night sky and seeing stars the way they were many years ago. Search results don't look that far back in time,

but a search engine may only refresh its information every few days, and the website could have changed since then.

You have still got a good chance of getting to what you wanted, though. Go back to the search results and look for the word "Cached" towards the end of the particular result you are using. Here is a full search result using the search **caleb simper**:

Church music – **Caleb Simper**
I'll be quite honest, **Caleb Simper** is not the usual sort of composer you would expect to find . . . But the fascination of **Caleb Simper** is his invisibility . . .
www.cul.co.uk/music/compx.htm – 61k – <u>Cached</u> – <u>Similar pages</u>

The "Cached" link is near the end, just before "Similar pages" (this is a facility that attempts to find related pages, but is usually too clever for its own good and doesn't work very well).

A cache is computer-speak for somewhere to store something away for a rainy day. In this case, the search engine kept a copy of the page it indexed, so even if it has disappeared from the web, you can click on the "Cached" link and see what it says. The cache isn't as good as the original – there are no pictures, for example – but it is much better than nothing, and even highlights the words you were searching for to make them easier to spot.

If you still can't find the text you're looking for in the cached version, then it really has disappeared, or it was never there – some web pages are good at fooling search engines into thinking they contain more information than they really do.

Checking the results

Let's take a look at a couple of search results from some of the other example searches we first met in chapter 2.

*Leland Stanford, founder of Stanford University, once bet on a flying horse.
Or did he? Explain.*

Our first suggestion was to take a look at **leland stanford biography**.
Here are some possible results:

Search on leland stanford biography

*Note that these are not real websites, just an idea of what you might
get. Most of the part of the result with the website name, cached
link, etc. that you would normally see in results has been omitted so
we can concentrate on the parts that matter.*

1   **Leland Stanford** . . . was an American business
    tycoon, politician and founder of Stanford
    University According to http://en.wikipedia.org/wiki/
    Leland Stanford

2   PBS – BIG MEN – **Leland Stanford** Photo of **Leland
    Stanford Leland Stanford**. (1824–1893). A member of the
    "Big Four" responsible for the Central Pacific railroad to
    California, **Leland Stanford** was a . . . *www.pbs.org*

3   **Leland Stanford** "Beyond Capitalism: **Leland Stanford**'s
    Forgotten Vision," by Lee Altenberg **Biography** of **Leland
    Stanford** from **Stanford** University . . . *www.sfmuseum.org*

    4   A visit to the **Leland Stanford** Mansion – 1881
        Leland Stanford's wife spent a huge amount of
        time and effort, especially before the birth of **Leland**
        Junior . . .

5   **STANFORD, Leland** – Biographical Information
    STANFORD, Leland, this Californian senator and
    later governor was born in . . . American Dictionary of
    Biography; Leland Stanford. . . . *bioguide.congress.gov*

    6   McNARY, Charles Linza – Biographical
        Information . . . 1874; the local school and then to
        Leland Stanford Junior University, . . . this is unlikely
        to have had any major impact on the **biography** . . .

> 7   Governor **Leland Stanford** of California **Leland Stanford**. Republican and 8th Governor of California from 1862 to 1863. – Short **Biography** – Birth – The Railroad – Living in 19th century California. **Biography** * . . . *www. governor.ca.gov*
>
> 8   **Leland Stanford** The All American Dictionary of Biography, . . . STANFORD, Leland, senator and governor, born at Watervliet, New York, www.americansyouve heardof.com . . .

What would you do, faced with these results? Spend a moment or two looking across them, and decide which results you would look at first.

Here's what I would do. The first entry is a special one, providing a link to the Wikipedia online encyclopedia (this is a real link that I've put in for you to try), and doesn't appear in the normal search result format. An encyclopedia is a great way to get a quick overview, so I would almost certainly take a look at this entry. Wikipedia can be very good. But bear in mind, as you'll discover on pages 51 and 84, that anyone can edit Wikipedia at any time. If someone does something stupid to it, like changing Stanford's dates or place of birth, the chances are that very soon someone else will fix the change. But the fact remains that at any one time, some of the entries in Wikipedia will have been interfered with and changed to false information, and others would have been filled in by visitors who actually don't know the facts.

Wikipedia is a great place to get some ideas, but you should never take the information in Wikipedia as definitive without checking it against a number of other sources.

The second entry takes us to a site of a TV broadcaster – the US public broadcaster, PBS. Sites run by respected broadcasters like PBS and the BBC usually provide good, reliable information, though they tend not to have a lot of detail, unless they are covering a news item or something similar. This would be a good site to read first to get a quick picture of Stanford before plunging into more detail.

The third entry sounds a bit too specific – it seems to be an academic paper on Stanford even though it does mention a biography. Still, it would be worth investigating.

Entry number four is indented. This means it's a different page at the same site as the previous entry. Again, it might be interesting, but is a bit too detailed for the moment, and seems to be about Stanford's house, not about the man. I can guess that both these entries come from the San Francisco museum from the start of the URL www.sfmuseum.org, so they are likely to be reliable.

Next up at number five we have another short biography, this time from the US Congress website – again, likely to be a reliable source and good as a starting point. But I can ignore entry 6, another biography at the same site, which seems to have been pulled up simply because the man in question attended Leland Stanford Junior University (the proper name of what is usually called Stanford University). This is a red herring.

Item 7 is not unlike number 5 – again, probably a short biography from a respectable site. Finally we get a site that might be useful, but isn't quite so certain in its source. Have I heard of this *Dictionary of Biography*? If so, it may be worth checking out for a bit more detail, but I would tread a little more cautiously.

All in all, a good set of responses there, and there would be plenty more to check out in a full search result. I'd probably take around the first fifty and scan them, following up maybe 10 of these.

Let's now look at another of the search results from chapter 2.

Write a 1,500 word essay, including diagrams, on fictional matter transmitters and real life quantum teleportation.

One of our suggested searches was quantum teleportation. Here are some results:

Search on quantum teleportation

Note that these are not real websites, just an idea of what you might get. Most of the part of the result with the website name, cached link, etc. that you would normally see in results has been omitted so we can concentrate on the parts that matter.

1   IBM: **Quantum Teleportation** Recent developments in **quantum** physics arising from entanglement, the phenomenon . . . *www.research.ibm.com* . . .

---

2   **Quantum Teleportation** What is **Quantum Teleporta-tion**? It's useful to see an experiment that shows . . .
www.its.caltech.edu

3   **Quantum teleportation** – Wikipedia, the free ency-clopedia **Quantum teleportation** sounds more impressive . . . when a particle undergoes **teleportation**. . . . . . .
en.wikipedia.org

4   **Quantum teleportation** evidence   perhaps the best evidence for survival of the soul comes from recent work in **quantum** physics . . . **teleportation** could be experienced after death . . . *www.mystobrain.com/psychic.html*

5   **Teleportation:** the **quantum** leap – one small step for a photon, but a leap for **quantum** science . . . **teleportation** across the laboratory . . . *news.nationalgeographic.com*

6   Physics > **Quantum Teleportation** in the Yahoo! Directory – Yahoo! reviewed these sites and found them related to Physics > **Quantum Teleportation**.

7   **Quantum teleportation** of rubidium clouds – **Quantum** teleportation can act not only on individual atoms but on atomic clouds . . . **quantum** effects in a Bose Einstein condensate . . . *www.nature.com*

8   BBC NEWS | Science/Nature | **Teleportation** goes long distance – the **quantum** phenomenon entanglement . . . Einstein called "spooky action at a distance" . . . pro-duce effects that are being used in **quantum** computers, and in **teleportation** of . . . *news.bbc.co.uk*

9   Cool techie stuff . . . best is **quantum teleportation**, which is so cool it's **quantum** frigid . . . I want to buy one! . . . *www.geocities.com/cooltech*

Again, spend a moment checking through these results and decide what you would like to explore first, what will give a good overview, what will give future leads, what is going to be in-depth and what could be on the flaky side.

Made your assessment? If not, go back and do it before you read on.

Okay. The first entry is from computer giant IBM, a respected company in the research field, so worth checking out to get some background. When getting information from a company you always have to be aware that there may be some bias – the company wants to look good – but where a company is talking about a speciality area, and not selling a product, as is the case here, they can provide excellent information.

Result number 2 is from Caltech, the California Institute of Technology – that's a good starting point, and it's describing an experiment to help understand what teleportation is about. This might be quite a technical site, but worth checking out.

The third result is a little like that first one in our previous search, but for some reason this time Wikipedia hasn't come up as a special entry. Again, useful background but bear in mind the warning about Wikipedia's reliability.

Entry 4 has the words we are looking for, but there are a few things about it that make me doubt it is going to be useful. It's from a rather odd sounding site and seems to be assuming some sort of crossover between quantum teleportation and mystic beliefs. Probably worth avoiding.

Items 5 and 8 are from respectable publications/broadcasters, in this case National Geographic and the BBC – both usually excellent to get a quick background view before plunging in with a bit more depth.

The sixth result is a link to another search engine – Yahoo – but here to the directory part, which has been edited by human beings, and has a section on quantum teleportation. That will provide us with another list of sites, and is well worth following up in a second pass through the information to get more pages to check out.

Number 7 is from *Nature*, one of the big science journals. Publications like *Nature* and *Science* have reader-friendly parts that give news about developments, and less reader-friendly papers that are in detailed science speak and often assume you know a lot about the subject. Still, it would be worth following this up on a second pass to see if you can get a little more detail without being blinded by science.

The final result looks like an individual's comments on teleportation, both from the wording and the site address on geocities. Chances are this isn't going to be useful.

One last thing worth pursuing. Did you notice a new keyword that will be worth following up? If not, take a quick look back over the results.

The word "entanglement" crops up a couple of times in a way that suggests it is fundamental to quantum teleportation, so I would add **entanglement** to my search plan, to find out more about what's going on.

You get the idea. You might like to try a couple of the other sample topics from chapter two – or one of your own. Take on a real search engine, and try to identify the most useful results, and any other search phrases to use, before clicking any of the result links. How did you do?

❗ Hot tip – it's not all HTML

We've looked at how to scan through the results of a search query and pick out the responses most likely to be useful, but there's another check you need to be doing as you work your way through those results. Most of the links you see will be to other web pages – ordinary HTML – but in principle they could be to any kind of computer file. Here are some of the more common results that aren't web pages:

[PDF] Communicating science
File Format: PDF/Adobe Acrobat – View as HTML

This search result indicates that the result is an Adobe Acrobat file (often called a PDF after the extension used in the filename). This is a special type of file that makes it possible to read and sometimes print a document, as it was intended to look, on most types of computer. It is usually produced from a word processor document. Like most of the special file formats, there are three ways to deal with a PDF:

- **Click on the link** If your browser has an add-in to view PDFs it will download the file and you can view it inside the browser. It can take a while for the first page to appear as you have to wait for the whole file to download and they can be quite big. If you haven't got an add-in you will be prompted to get one.

- **Click on View as HTML** This shows an attempt Google makes to translate the PDF file into an ordinary web page. These are of mixed quality, depending on the complexity of the PDF. Some are almost as good as the original, others a mess. It's worth a try if you only want some text, rather than the whole look of the thing, as it can be much quicker than waiting for a PDF file to download.
- **Right click the link and select Save Target As . . . or Save Link As . . .** You can then save the PDF file onto your PC and read it there. Mac users should hold down the control key and click the link to pop up the menu. This is often better than trying to read it within your browser. You will need a (free) copy of Adobe Acrobat Reader to read the file. If you haven't got one, it can be downloaded from www.adobe.com

[PPT] The Art Files
File Format: Microsoft PowerPoint 97 – View as HTML

Here we've got a PowerPoint presentation. You will often see these where the search result is linked to a lecture or talk. Again, you can download it, view it within your browser if it has a viewer add-in, or see Google's attempt at turning it into HTML. Because PowerPoint is usually used for the slides in a presentation, the text is often pretty meaningless without the talk it was supposed to accompany, so PowerPoint presentations are often best avoided.

[DOC] Living History
File Format: Microsoft Word 2000 – View as HTML

You may also come across documents from a word processor, most often saved in Microsoft Word. Again, the three possibilities apply. Viewing as HTML tends to be more successful with Word documents than with some of the more visual formats, so it's usually worth a try.

Keeping track of results

When you are doing a first quick check through the sites that you have discovered in your search, it can be really useful (especially if you have a decent sized monitor) to pop the results up in separate windows on your screen. You can do this by making a change in the search engine's preferences as we saw on page 25, or by right clicking the link (control click on Macs), instead of a normal left click, and choosing **Open (Link) in New Window** from the menu that pops up.

An alternative approach is to use a web browser that supports tabbed results. If you are using a version of Internet Explorer older than version 7 consider either upgrading to the latest version (see www.microsoft.com), or try out the rival Firefox browser (see www. mozilla.com/firefox). Both these browsers allow you to keep a range of web pages open at once, each identified by a tab. This makes it easy to flick quickly between them – great when checking through search results.

! Hot tip – Where was I?

One of the disadvantages of using the web is the sheer volume of material you can get through. You may be working on a project and suddenly realize that you saw just the right thing a couple of days ago . . . but where was it? You can't remember. Luckily, your browser can help you out. Check out the history list (on Internet Explorer obtained by clicking the button with a green arrow turning back the clock; on Firefox it's the clock button or History from the Go menu).

If you know *when* you saw the page, use the View drop down in the History panel that pops up to display the information by date and see a list of the sites you visited (if it wasn't long ago you'd do better with the "by order visited today" option). Alternatively use the Search option within the History panel to look for keywords that will identify the page you were looking at. You'll be back there in no time.

When you have your search results, even if you've just got a single page, it might be difficult to find the actual bit of text you were looking for – especially if it's a long page and the item appears well down it. Many web pages are designed to only take up a screen or two, but others can have hundreds or even thousands of lines of text. As there's no enforced limit, in principle a single web page could be an entire book.

Never mind: you can always search inside your search. All browsers have a search facility (usually called something like "find in this page" under the Edit menu) to track down a specific bit of text. This is one job where the Firefox browser really shines. Its "find in page" facility is excellent. It sits conveniently at the bottom of the page out of the way rather than being a box that sits on top of the text you are looking at, it highlights the term you are looking for, making it easy to find, and it searches as you type, so you know immediately if there's anything there.

Specific searches – finding book contents

At any one time there are around two million books in print in the English language. That's all the books that you can order from a bookstore or online. And there are plenty more titles that aren't for sale any more. Of those books in print, the majority are in copyright. This means that the author is alive, or died some time in the last 70 years. When a book is in copyright, it's illegal to make your own copy of it, or to reproduce large chunks of it, to protect the author's livelihood (if the author is dead it's their estate that is being protected).

You are allowed to make use of small pieces of the text to illustrate a point – the rules vary from country to country, but the general rule is that while text is in copyright, you can publish a small snippet to illustrate something without the copyright holder's consent – but you mustn't pass it off as your own work, and you can only use a relatively small part of the work, whatever it is – so if it's a ten-line poem, you are much more limited than with a full size book. Of course, if all you are doing is copying some text to refer to in a school assignment there shouldn't be any problem (as long as you make clear where it came from).

Once those 70 years expire, though, and the book goes out of copyright, it's a free-for-all. Anyone can copy as much of the text as they like. This is why there are so many cheap "classic" books on sale – publishers can print them whenever they like and don't have to pay the author anything. Over the last few years a great many such books have been scanned and are available online. We're not talking about little snippets here – the whole book from cover to cover can be browsed or copied. So if you need a quote from *Alice in Wonderland*, or to use a piece of Jane Austen's writing to illustrate a point, there's no need to hunt it down in the library and painfully copy it out by hand – you can go straight to the appropriate site and cut and paste to your heart's content, or download the whole thing for future use.

! Hot tip – eBook formats

Some of these online books are just a set of web pages to flip through in your browser, but this is very clumsy, so many more are held as eBooks – files you can download to your computer to read later. These come in a range of formats, including:

- **Text** – simple .txt files with no formatting. Fine for searching for a particular piece of text, but not particularly readable.
- **HTML** – web format files, with the layout controlled in the same way as a web page.
- **PDF/Acrobat** – Adobe Acrobat files, designed to give a good, clear page layout like a printed document on any major type of computer. If you haven't got it, you need to download the free Acrobat reader software from www.adobe.com
- **Adobe Reader** – a special variant of Acrobat, designed for commercial eBooks. The free reader has a lot of protection built in (whether you can copy the book, whether you can print it), and special versions of the software for reading on Palms and Pocket PC PDAs.
- **Microsoft Reader** – a similar idea to Adobe Reader, but you can't read an Adobe book with the Microsoft Reader, or vice versa. Again, designed for reading on

screen on anything from PDAs to PCs, and with strong copy and print protection.

- **Overdrive Audio Book** – a downloadable audio book format with similar controls to the Adobe and Microsoft readers for printed books.
- **Audible.com Audio Book** – another commercial audio book format, using iTunes style downloading to most standard computer/MP3 audio players.

Exactly how a scanned book appears online depends on the kind of book it is and the process involved. Some are simple text versions. Others are still in text that you can cut and paste but have all the formatting of a real book. Finally, for texts where the look of the original is important – for instance in providing a medieval manuscript to study – there may be a photographic reproduction of each page, which is great for getting that visual effect, but means you can't copy the text. Take a look at the Beinecke Rare Book and Manuscript Library at Yale University (beinecke.library.yale.edu/brbldl) to see this kind of online book.

This is a bumper time for projects aiming to scan large quantities of printed books. A few sites have been available for many years, slowly and painfully adding a few books at a time, but the big players have now jumped in. Google, for instance, as well as having grandiose plans to scan every book in print, giving browsers the ability to see small fragments (see page 6), also has a link-up with several big name libraries, including Oxford University, Stanford and the New York Public Library to scan their contents and make the non-copyright books (and quite possibly others) available online.

! Hot tip – finding online books

Here's where to find the best selection of books on the web:

- **Google Print Library Project** (books.google.com)
  This site has a huge amount of information, but the big

disadvantage is that you can only search, there is no index to look up a particular author or book. If, for example, you search for **"james joyce" ulysses** you will get lots of references to books that talk about Joyce, and samples from printed editions of *Ulysses*, but it could take you a while to find the actual text. You can limit the date of publication in the advanced book search, to omit in-copyright books they'll want you to pay for.

- **Project Gutenberg** (www.gutenberg.org) When I last looked, this free facility had passed the 17,000 books mark, and it has the advantage of having both an index and a search facility. The books are for download, rather than reading direct on the web. They may be in plain text, HTML, PDF, or a more obscure format, and some are ZIP files (compressed) to make the download smaller. Windows XP and later users can open these as if they were folders – with other operating systems you might need to download a small unzipping utility.

- **The Universal Library** (www.ulib.org) This is a mega scheme, with an initial target of one million out of copyright books scanned, and the aim to have 10 million books on the database ten years after that. The access currently offers a search by title and author, or a free search of any text in the books, and wasn't working properly last time I tried it. This site is still in the early development stages at the time of writing.

- **Bibliomania** (www.bibliomania.com) Bibliomania is a collection of classic (including relatively modern classic) fiction, plays and poetry. Readable on-screen and can be copied as text. Also has a section of study guides, and a section of classic reference books.

- **Digital Book Index** (www.digitalbookindex.org) This site provides a handy index of over 100,000

online books and will find a mix of free books and
eBooks still in copyright, which you can buy.

- **eBooklocator** (www.ebooklocator.com) Although
rather clumsy at the time of writing, it has a good
listing of commercial eBooks to buy from different
sources. Once you have found a book you have to click
through to a retailer, find it again, and buy it.
- **Bartleby** (www.bartleby.com) This is the grand-
daddy of online book sites. Looking round Bartleby is
like strolling around the library in an old house. There
are plenty of classics from Shakespeare to Thomas
Mallory, and some solid (if venerable) reference
books. All the content is directly accessed as a web
page, so it's great if you want to copy the text of a
Burns poem or a well-known quotation, but not so
good for actually reading a book cover to cover.
- **Internet Archive** (www.archive.org) Perhaps the
strangest of the online archives, giving access to a
mix of moving images, music, audio, and texts.
Provides an interface to the Million Book Project from
the Universal Library, Project Gutenberg and more.
Also includes the WayBackMachine, which contains
40 billion archived web pages. Includes free audio
versions of books from the LibriVox site (www.
librivox.org).
- **The Online Books Page** (digital.library.upenn.edu/
books) The University of Pennsylvania's online library
is the other grand old man of online books sites.
Not huge by modern standards (around 25,000
books). Mostly points to books at other sites like
Project Gutenberg and Bartleby. Interesting News
section that gives information on the latest online
book developments.
- **MSN Book Search** (accessed via www.msn.com)
Working with the Open Content Alliance (www.
opencontentalliance.org) and Internet Archive, this

is another site with the intention of a grand book scanning process to make information more widely available. Not up and running at the time of going to press.

The range of books available on these sites is increasingly impressive. Whether you want to check the text of James Joyce's *Ulysses* or to explore Harvey's original *On the Motion of the Heart and Blood in Animals*, you can find it out there.

Specific searches – finding actual books

So the book you want isn't online. What next? You may have to take the trip to the library, but the web can still come in handy. Your school or university library may have an online catalog – see for example Oxford University's online library catalog at www.lib.ox.ac.uk/olis or Stanford University's at library.stanford.edu/catdb You can find the catalog of a site by doing a web search on the institution's name and library, or by going to the school's website and looking for, or searching for, library. You will also find online catalogs of other big libraries, such as the New York Public Library (www.nypl.org) or the British Library (www.bl.uk), which incidentally has a bizarre, non-standard URL.

Your own local library may well also have its catalogs online. Try searching for the place name plus **library**, or take a look at your local government website, which will probably have a section on library services. If it doesn't, it is still worth using one of the big library catalogs above to find the details of the book before you go into your library and ask for a particular book. That way you can give the librarian details like date of publication and ISBN, making it quicker and easier to find the book you want. Even if your local library doesn't hold a copy, they will usually have arrangements (called Inter-library Loan in the UK) to have the book brought in from another library, though there may be a charge for this.

> ## ❗ Hot tip – using ISBN
>
> All books currently in print, and most of the books printed in the last 40 years or so have an ISBN (International Standard Book Number). This is a definitive way to identify a particular book, so it's useful to make a note of it. An ISBN is a string of numbers that usually appears on the back cover of the book, and always on the page that has the copyright details. It looks something like this: 0749429496, though it may be shown with gaps between some of the digits, like a telephone number. Don't worry if the last digit is a letter X – it's not a misprint, it is allowed.
>
> Books printed before 2007 had 10-digit ISBNs, but more recent titles will have a 13-digit number. All library catalogs and online booksellers like Amazon include the ISBN in their listing. The only thing to watch out for is that ISBNs change if there is a different edition of the book. A single book may have half a dozen different ISBNs for hardback, paperback, second edition, and so forth.

There is another way to get hold of books for research – buy them. This might seem a very expensive way to get an assignment done, but if it's a big project it may be worth it, and it doesn't have to be expensive. In fact you can often resell your books for as much as you bought them for after you have used them.

To keep costs down, use a secondhand source like the Marketplace section of Amazon (www.amazon.com/www.amazon.co.uk), or Abebooks (www.abebooks.com/www.abebooks.co.uk). Abebooks is a pure secondhand source, but it is probably worth starting with Amazon. Look up the book as you normally would on Amazon, searching on Books to cut down the results. On the right hand of the page you will see a Marketplace box, labeled something like "more buying choices" and listing how many new and used copies are available. You can usually buy a book cheaper than the full price, then use the same Marketplace feature to sell the book when you are finished with it (go to the book's page and click on "sell your book here" to list it).

Don't assume Marketplace will always be cheapest – check Amazon's own price (or whichever online retailer you prefer) as well. And consider buying new if you expect to keep the book. But as a library substitute, buying and reselling second hand can be surprisingly cost effective (you might even make a profit!).

Specifics – the rest

There are plenty of other specifics you might need to search for. We'll cover media – music, images, video – in the next chapter, but that's only the beginning.

Most importantly, the web is a good source for basic facts – information that you frequently need to deal with homework or a project. This is the stuff you would traditionally go to an encyclopedia, a dictionary, or a similar reference book for. You will find online versions of many of the old standards at some of the book sites above (www.bartleby.com, for instance), but there are also reference works with more friendly interfaces. So let's take a look at the usual suspects of quick reference.

What does a word mean?

Time to reach for the dictionary. If you are lucky you will get a definition, how the word evolved and some examples of using it. You may also get a pronunciation guide, either using the messy phonetic symbols, or better by clicking on a button and listening to it. Try:

- www.dictionary.com – easy to remember, with content from American Heritage Dictionary and Webster's (US spellings).
- www.askoxford.com – online access to the Compact Oxford Dictionary, the pocket dictionary from OUP (UK spellings).
- www.m-w.com – online dictionary from Merriam-Webster, one of the top US reference publishers (US spellings).
- encarta.msn.com – click on the dictionary link at the top to search this large online dictionary (US spellings, but has many of the UK variants).
- www.oed.com – probably the greatest of all English dictionaries, you can access the Oxford English Dictionary online, but only if you are a subscriber. Luckily libraries can subscribe on your behalf – ask at your local library or school/university library, they may have a subscription (UK and US spellings).

Who said this?

There's nothing like a quotation to add a touch of class to a piece of work, and chances are someone has already said something appropriate. Paper dictionaries of quotations are irritatingly messy to use – this is an ideal subject to approach online.

- www.askoxford.com – online access to the Little Oxford Dictionary of Quotations. You may need to select "quotations dictionary" from the drop down box.
- www.bartleby.com – the online book source has a reference section where you can search three dictionaries of quotations including the venerable Bartlett's, but also the modern Columbia (and other reference books too).

What would this be in French?

Or any other language you need to know about. Don't expect an online translation facility to do your homework for you – the translations are rough at best – but it's a great way to check what a word means or to get an idea of what a piece of text in a foreign language is about.

- www.google.com or www.google.co.uk – click on Language Tools on the main page. A translation box lets you translate between English and a range of other languages. Also translates foreign language web pages.
- world.altavista.com – the Alta Vista search engine was the first to offer online translation, and its Babel Fish translator is still one of the best. Includes more languages than Google, and has an on-screen keyboard to handle Russian characters.
- www.freetranslation.com – a similar facility to Google, but includes a few extra languages.

Can you give me a quick summary of this subject?

Sometimes you don't want to work through a lot of different web pages on a topic, you just want a quick summary. Encyclopedias are great for this.

- www.wikipedia.org – on some subjects (science is particularly strong) this is the best of all the online encyclopedias. Its unique feature is its greatest strength and greatest weakness. Anyone (you, for instance) can change any of the text at any time. This means lots of different experts can refine the content – but also that when you look up a subject it could just have been changed to something silly. Do use it, but check it against another source before relying on it.

- **encarta.msn.com** – the slickest of the online encylopedias with a wealth of content – well worth trying. Has a premium (subscription) version with even more information.
- **www.britannica.com** – the most famous traditional printed reference book, Encyclopedia Britannica offers a small part of its content free, but you have to subscribe to get the full thing.
- **www.encyclopedia.com** – 57,000 articles from the Columbia Encyclopedia. Better than the childish look of the site implies. The articles are text only unless you go for the premium (subscription) High Beam service.

What other words can I use?

Fed up of with saying something is "nice" all the time? You could try admirable, agreeable, amiable, attractive, charming, commendable, delightful, friendly, good, gracious, groovy, kind, lovely, peachy . . . and many others, thanks to a thesaurus.

- **www.thesaurus.com** – the same people who run dictionary.com have an online version of Roget's New Millennium Thesaurus.
- **www.m-w.com** – online thesaurus from Merriam-Webster, one of the top US reference publishers.
- **encarta.msn.com** – click on the thesaurus link at the top to access an effective if sometimes compact thesaurus.

What's in the news?

Finding information on a topical subject is easy with a host of sites from TV news shows and newspapers worldwide. Try a source outside your own country as well as a familiar one to get a broader viewpoint. Here are just a few options (you can find any favorite with a search engine):

- **news.bbc.co.uk** – probably the best known news service in the world, from the very effective BBC news team.

- **www.cnn.com** – worldwide coverage with a US flavor from CNN.
- **news.google.com** or **news.google.co.uk** – a news *aggregator*, pulling together news from a wide range of sources.
- **www.nytimes.com** – online version of this famous paper.
- **www.washingtonpost.com** – another great US paper online.
- **www.times.co.uk** – the best known of the British newspapers.
- **www.guardian.co.uk** – two British newspapers (the *Guardian* and the *Observer*) at a single site.

Smart searching – essentials

If you search smart, you are much more likely to get to useful results quickly.

- Guess the obvious sites – if you are looking for the Microsoft site, for instance, it's worth guessing www.microsoft.com before bothering with a search engine.
- Make use of special formats like putting phrases in double blips, adding meaning with round brackets and using keywords like OR and NOT.
- Try out a meta search engine and see if it works for you.
- Practice scanning the results, looking for the most likely candidates.
- Look out for frequently repeated words in the results, which might provide new keywords.
- Keep track of results by putting them in separate pages or (better) using a browser with tabbed pages.
- Make use of online books.
- Use the web as a route to get to real books too.
- Use quick reference sources (dictionary, thesaurus, encyclopedia, etc.) for the types of information they are designed for – they will be quicker and more useful than doing a general search if you want the definition of a word or another quick reference function.

Chapter 4

Amassing media

Here are a couple of irritating old sayings about pictures – "Every picture tells a story," and "A picture is worth a thousand words." Okay, maybe they are irritating, but there's a grain of truth in there. You can put a lot across with a good picture. Sometimes it makes your text easier to understand. Sometimes it just makes the presentation look more attractive. Either way, a good picture is well worth including, and the web is the perfect place to find it. It is also a good source for many other media formats, from sheet music to video – and we'll cover all of these in this chapter.

Picture this

The search engines go out of their way to make finding images easy for you. Each of our recommended search engines has a link on the home page called "images" or "pictures" that takes you to a search page solely for finding photographs and drawings. Put in a search term in the usual way and you will get a collection of thumbnail pictures to choose from.

As usual, you can save yourself from wasting a lot of time if you don't jump in straight away to the first picture you see. Some of the pictures that have been found will be no bigger than the little thumbnail you see. Others may be much more detailed and larger. If all you want is a small picture to act as a border illustration, or your own thumbnail, you won't mind a small image, but if you want to use the image big enough to fill half a page or more, to show all the detail you will need a larger image.

Most of the image searches will give you the choice of seeing all pictures or just small, medium, or large, making it easier to pick out what you want. If you have a broadband connection and you don't want many images, you might as well get large pictures, but they can be slow to download, and there will be more choice of small images – many websites don't have images beyond a certain size.

Take a look at the search result before making a choice. It will show the size of the image in pixels (the individual little colored blocks that make up the image) and in bytes. For instance, it might say "640×480 pixels 31k". By modern standards this is an acceptable but smallish photograph. If you want really good detail, look for something around the 800×600 mark or bigger. Note that the size of the file (31 kilobytes in the example above) isn't directly linked to the image size in pixels, as most images are JPG files, which have different amounts of compression to squeeze the image into a small file. But, again, the file size will give you a rough feel for whether you are dealing with a tiny image or a good-sized one.

> ## ! Hot tip – safe searches
>
> You can't avoid the fact that the web has some sites that maybe you don't particularly want to search. When it comes to photographs, it's particularly easy to stray into sites with images that either aren't relevant, or are pretty gross. Most search engines have a "safe search" option that tries to limit the unwanted sites. This may well be switched on already, but check in the search engine's preference page. Going for safe search will give you a better match to your requirement. It's not perfect – it isn't going to stop every doubtful page – but it is worth using.

You aren't going to be able to tell for sure whether a picture is just what you need without seeing the real thing (some of them won't even be there any more). Clicking on the thumbnail will usually take you to a page that combines the thumbnail at the top with the source page below, where you can see the full picture.

You can at this stage just copy the picture directly from the web browser and paste it into your word processor. Right click the picture (click with the control key held down on a Mac) and select copy, then switch to the word processor and paste (remember, the quick key way to do this is Ctrl-V), but this is often not the best way to handle a picture. Instead it can be useful to save it to your PC, get a collection of pictures together first and then place them in your document.

Saving the image is easy. Right click the picture on screen (control click on a Mac) and select "Save Image as . . .", or with Internet Explorer click on the disc icon in the little bar that pops up when your mouse is over the picture. Unless you are building a large library (in which case it's worth having a separate folder to keep them in), you might want to just save the pictures on your desktop while you work with them.

If you are using Word or a program like OneNote or Mind Manager to organize your work, you can quickly put together a collection of your images by dragging the file you have saved onto the program. Alternatively, make sure you give each picture a name that is meaningful to you and put them straight from your desktop into the project.

Not every picture will be exactly as you want it to appear – but it takes very little time to work a picture into shape. Resizing is simply a matter of dragging the handles (the little black squares at the edges of the picture when it is selected) to get it to the size you want. To keep the picture in proportion, only use the handles on the corners. If you want to trim off some of the picture, keeping it the same size, use a crop tool instead. In Word, the easiest way is to open the picture toolbar (it may open automatically when you click on the picture – alternatively, right click/control click the toolbars at the top and select the picture toolbar).

The standard icon for a cropping tool will look something like this:

Once the crop tool is selected, the handles will trim off the edges of the image without shrinking the overall picture.

Positioning the image is also flexible, depending on the word processor. In Word, double click the image to control sizing, borders and more. Perhaps the most useful tab on this dialog box is for layout. Use this to position the image on the page, rather than have it sit in line with the text as if it were another text character.

Of course you are not limited to the way an image looks when you get it from the internet. Even a simple editing program can do anything from tone down red eye in a photograph to combining elements from different pictures on a single image. This isn't the place to give a lesson in using a graphics package, but with a bit of practice you can enhance images quickly and effectively to give a better result.

> **! Hot tip - cloning and toning**
>
> If you do decide to make use of a graphics package to improve an image, perhaps the most useful tool is a cloning brush. This lets you take a part of the image and blend a copy of it into another part of the picture. While the obvious thing you can do is to make a copy of something (look, two of me!), it is most useful for clearing up blemishes. If the original picture has an unwanted blob or crease, you can clone nearby blank space over the mark to erase it invisibly.
>
> Another facility in most graphics packages is the ability to tone a picture – to change it from full color into an image that (for example) is primarily blue. This is great if you want to use the image for a title page or as a graphic divider, rather than as a straightforward illustration. Toning the picture will give it a much more sophisticated look. Look for controls in the program that let you modify color, hue, and tone.

Think a little before modifying a picture. It is possible to produce an image this way that is a visual lie, a misrepresentation of the facts. This might be convenient to get a message across, but it is rarely what's wanted in good work.

Most images from the web will be in color – and why not, so is the world. But don't assume just because you've got color images you need to print everything in color. For many assignments a black and white print is just as effective, and it will cost you a lot less, particularly if you have access to a laser printer. Like any use of color, color printing is great to highlight something, but if over-used can result in a mess. Use color to highlight, or if the color in an illustration is significant, rather than purely for the sake of it. Keep the main text to black. If you want color but also to keep cost down, only print the pages with color on the color printer.

Whose picture is it anyway?

Like most of the material on the web, the copyright of pictures is usually owned by the person who created it, or the website owner. With text, you normally won't have a problem with this, as you won't often be copying the text word for word (see chapter 8), but pictures are more likely to be lifted straight off a web page and dropped into your assignment.

Technically, by doing this you are probably breaking the copyright laws. If the piece of work is only a school assignment to be marked and thrown away, there isn't a lot of risk attached to doing this. But do watch out if the work you are doing is for a competition, or anything that could be subsequently published in any way (including on your school's website). Under those circumstances it's important to get permission to reproduce the image.

Look for an email address on the website you got the image from (or the publisher's website if you are scanning the image from a book or postcard), and send them a short email requesting permission to reproduce the image, telling them what it's for and where it's likely to appear. Something like this:

Hello,

I would like permission to reproduce the image [filename] from your web page [web page] in my school project on football. A single copy will be printed for assessment and destroyed afterwards. The project may be displayed on a school notice-board and the school website (www. myschool.edu). I would be grateful if you could let me know if this is okay by [date], as I have to hand in my assignment then. Thanks very much.

Yours,

(Your name)

Ideally you should allow them around two weeks to reply. If you don't get a reply (and this happens quite often), send a second email, forwarding the first, like this:

Hello,

I emailed you on [date], requesting permission to reproduce an image in my school project. (See below for original email.) I do need to get my assignment handed in, and haven't heard from you yet. Unless I hear from you by [date] I will assume that you have given permission to reproduce the image. Thanks for your help.

Etc . . .

Again, you should ideally leave another week before assuming permission. This doesn't give you legal permission to copy, but it would be difficult for the copyright holder to accuse you of taking a copy without permission if they don't respond.

It's best to print off and keep copies of these emails.

Get the picture

Let's do some practical picture searching for two of our sample assignments. In the big project we needed a cover page and illustrations around the subject of Roger Bacon.

Most of the pictures I found in a quick search were black and white – either drawn portraits of Roger or statues. I could use one of these on the title page, but it would be nice to give it some color, using the toning techniques mentioned above. Because Roger lived in medieval times, I might decide to make the cover look a bit like a medieval illuminated manuscript. I could take an image of a manuscript and use a cloning brush to add one of the pictures of Bacon into it, then type over my own title.

I would also be looking for illustrations of the sort of work that Roger did, and about his life. So as I found out more, I would be looking for pictures of Oxford and Paris in the 1200s, for the living conditions of Franciscan friars back then, and for scenes featuring the work of medieval scientists.

For our visual guide we needed to find three Manet paintings and to provide an illustrated guide for a tour of the locations. I might start with a search on **manet painting**. As we want to do a location based project, I would discount the pure portraits like *Olympia*. Because Manet's style is quite distinct, I also need to be on the lookout for Manet pastiches – pretend paintings that look like Manet did them but aren't really by him. When I did a search, the results included "Manet's Painting of Kelly Osbourne". The picture of the rock star's daughter and reality TV celebrity might have been in a kind-of-Manet style, but it was certainly no Manet original.

I might settle on Manet's *On the Beach*, his *Gare St. Lazare* and his *Bar at The Folies Bergere*. Now I have my locations. I would want decent sized images of each of these paintings, but then I would look for pictures of the places. I would need to find them on a map (and include that map in my project – see page 63). There would also be a bit of detective work. The painting *On the Beach* is clearly at the seaside, and very probably the French seaside, but I would need to track down exactly where by reading information on Manet at different sites. In this, rather different, style of assignment, the pictures drive the whole structure and so I need to assemble some pictures before I get any further.

Making music

You might have heard the quotation "music soothes the savage beast", and if you look that phrase up on a search engine you will find plenty of references. Unfortunately it's a misquote, and if you use Bartleby instead (see page 46) you will find that the actual words are "Music has charms to soothe a savage *breast*" – no beasts involved.

Either way, music is a powerful thing. What is it, when you're watching a movie, that brings a lump to your throat or starts the tears flowing? It's that sudden surge of dramatic music. Our brains are wired up to respond to music emotionally and music can be useful beyond the obvious applications of a music project to illustrate work in other subjects.

It's hard not to have come across music downloads – originally from illegal file sharing and more recently from online music stores like iTunes. It is possible you might want to make use of music downloads in a project – perhaps to hear a piece of music you have to comment on – but it is more likely that you will make use of MIDI files which have the distinct advantage of usually being free.

MIDI?

MIDI stands for Musical Instrument Device Interface. It was originally designed as a way of linking different musical instruments together so that you could play (for example) an electronic drumkit from a keyboard, or a whole band's worth of instruments from a computer. But at the heart of MIDI is a set of simple instructions that tell an electronic instrument what to sound like and what notes to play. Because MIDI files are just basic information (like play middle C for one second) rather than a recording, they are tiny compared with MP3 and other music download formats. Almost all computers can now play MIDI files, eliminating the need for a separate, MIDI-based musical instrument.

It probably isn't worth trying anything specialist to find MIDI files. Your usual search engine will do fine. Just put in the name of the song or piece and MIDI as the search term. This is an example where Google's + sign is useful. Normally, if you just enter MIDI in the search term, it will also show results with the word "mid" in them. But make it **+midi** and you won't have that problem (though if it's a classical piece you are looking for, you will probably accidentally throw up Debussy's *Prélude à l'Après-midi d'un Faune*).

You can then download any MIDIs in the result by clicking through to the page they are on and right clicking (Macs – control-click) the link to the file itself, which will end in .mid, and saving it on your computer. Alternatively, you can use a web link to the original file itself in your work (for example www.cul.co.uk/music/widor.mid) – the reader can use the link to hear the music themselves.

MIDI files have their limitations. There are no words, so even if it's a song, it will just be the tune. And they are very variable in quality. They might sound like a mechanical idiot picking out the tune badly with one finger on a wholly inappropriate instrument, or they might sound like a virtuoso performance – it depends on how well they are programmed.

> ## ! Hot tip – MIDIs and the law
>
> MIDI files occupy a gray area in the law. They aren't covered by the same sort of protection that a downloaded music file is, as no performer is going to lose out if you download a MIDI. It's really more like having a friend pick a tune out on a piano – you can't really license it.
>
> If you stick to the strict letter of the law, MIDI files probably breach copyright for any music where the composer is still alive, or died less than 70 years ago, as the MIDI file is effectively a version of the sheet music (though not one a normal person can read). However, you will find MIDI files of lots of songs and pieces that are protected stringently in other formats, so it seems that the music publishers are not too worried by them. For personal use, or for use in an assignment, there should not be a problem.

Music without sound

Sometimes you don't want to hear a tune, you want to see it. If getting your hands on sheet music is important to you, whether it's to play yourself for a music exam, or as part of the contents of a project on a composer, then the good news is that the web has plenty of free sheet music on offer.

Like books, sheet music is protected by copyright. If the composer is still alive, or died less than 70 years ago, then you can't freely copy his or her music unless they give explicit permission to do so. However, there are some very good sources of legitimate free sheet music on the web:

- **Free Sheet Music Net** (www.freesheetmusic.net) This is a good sized directory of free sheet music sites (a fair number of the sites listed do charge, but a significant proportion are free).
- **8 Notes** (www.8notes.com) This site contains listings of free sheet music on other sites, but also links to individual pieces, and includes a small amount of jazz and pop.
- **Musica Viva** (www.musicaviva.com) Musica Viva has a database

of free music on the site itself, plus links to other sheet music sites and a MIDI collection.

- **Choral Public Domain Library** (www.cpdl.org) Also called Choral Wiki, as it uses the Wikipedia software, though limited to choral music (sung music), this is a great place to look.

Online music is held in a number of formats. Perhaps most common is PDF (Acrobat) files, which can be looked at and printed on any computer. You will also find a fair number of scores simply scanned as an image – for example as a JPG file. Most versatile is Scorch, which is a file format specially designed for viewing and printing sheet music from a website. It is very flexible – if set up correctly you can, for instance, play the music on screen, and change the key of the music before printing it. You can get the Scorch plug-in from the Sibelius site www.sibeliusmusic.com

If the music you want isn't available for free, you may have to pay for it. If you just want a single piece you may be able to pay to download a copy from the web, getting instant access, but failing that, and certainly if you want a book, you are back to buying and waiting. There are plenty of sheet music sites out there – try www.musicroom.com (UK) and www.sheetmusicplus.com (US) for starters.

Moving pictures

Although you are relatively unlikely to want to include movies in an assignment, it is possible you may be able to submit some work electronically, and movies can be a very impressive supplement to a presentation you give to your class. If using movies this way, remember to keep the moving image simple and short. A few seconds' clip of a movie can be very effective to get your message across.

You may well find something by simply doing a normal search with **video** or **movie** in the keywords. Alternatively, Google is building a video archive at video.google.com Movies can be viewed on-screen, and some can be downloaded to watch on a computer, video iPod or PSP games console, making them more attractive for a presentation. As with most other media, commercial movies are copyright and it is illegal to download them, but you may find free clips – trailers, for instance – available from the movie's producers.

If you want to build a video into a Powerpoint presentation, it will need to be in AVI, Quicktime or MPG format – much of the video you find on the web will either be streaming video, designed to watch as a web page but not downloaded, or in a format that can't be built into your presentation, like Google's videos.

Of course, your interest could be in finding information on movies, rather than finding moving images. Most of the well-known movies will have sites dedicated to them, where you can collect plenty of information – find them using a standard web search – but it's always worth taking a look at the Internet Movie Database as a starting point. See www.imdb.com for a comprehensive listing of movies, actors and behind-the-scenes crew.

Mapping the world

The final but certainly not least significant media search is for maps. A map can be a great way to illustrate an event, to describe a journey or simply to let your audience know where a place is. Watch the way the TV news puts a location across. If they want to describe an event in Minsk, for instance, they will show a map of the world with the country Belarus highlighted, then zoom in to show the location of Minsk itself. If you are referring to a place in a non-fiction assignment, you will almost always benefit from a map that shows where it is.

The web can provide you with just as many types of map as you can imagine, but broadly they fall into three categories: an indicator map, which might just show the location of a town within the country, or could be used to identify political boundaries or information like levels of pollution; a direction map, which gives a lot more detail and will usually include roads; and a photographic map, an aerial photograph from satellite or plane that gives a view from above of the area in question.

Indicator maps are most likely to turn up in a general web search. The chances are that someone else has already wanted to (for instance) show where Belarus is in the world, so you can make use of their attempt. For direction maps, it is worth turning to a specialist site. In the UK, for example, there are two excellent mapping sites, Streetmap (www.streetmap.co.uk) and Multimap (www.multimap.com). Of these, Streetmap has the more flexible maps, while Multimap has the neat feature of being able to superimpose an aerial photograph on the map at detailed scale. It's also worth taking a look at the site of the Ordnance Survey, the UK's mapping body (www.ordancesurvey. co.uk).

You will find similar sites for many other countries. Try putting the country name and **mapping** into a search engine. Google and friends have also got in on the act. Google has mapping down to street level, and the ability to superimpose satellite imagery and route planning at maps.google.co.uk and maps.google.com Yahoo uses Map 24's mapping facilities at maps.yahoo.co.uk and maps.yahoo.com

Quite a few of the mapping sites incorporate aerial photographs taken from planes or satellites, but a final essential when looking for a photographic map-like view is Google Earth. This free software gives a visual overview of the whole Earth, with the ability to zoom in to any location. The quality of the pictures varies, depending on how well known the place is. Pick somewhere in the middle of nowhere and you will probably have to take the view up to around 20,000 feet to get a clear-looking picture. But over the center of New York or London, for instance, you can drop down to around 400 feet, clearly viewing not only cars and buses but individual people. Although Google Earth is a program rather than an image, you can save the current view (Save Image from the File menu) and then use it as normal. See earth.google.com for more information.

Maps, like any written document, are subject to copyright. You should not make copies and put them on a website or publish them in any way. However, though still technically not legal, it is very unlikely anyone is going to have a problem with a map from the internet being included in your homework assignment.

Amassing media – essentials

Pictures and other media content can transform a dull assignment into something much more attractive. Make sure that the illustrations you use are relevant, though. Don't use pictures just to fill up space.

- Use an image search to find appropriate illustrations.
- Keep an eye on the size information in the search results to choose suitable images.
- Be prepared to make some changes to your pictures – at the very least to resize and crop them – to best fit your project.
- MIDI files are easy to come by and can be very effective music sources.
- Make use of maps and satellite imagery to put locations in your assignment into context.

Chapter 5

Real people

The internet is a big place – and it's not all the web. There are real people out there who can prove to be unique sources of information. Asking for information can take considerably more time and effort than browsing a few websites, and for some of us it can be quite embarrassing, so chances are it's only appropriate for major pieces of work, but it can make all the difference. Get some input from the right real person and your assignment is going to have unique content that no one else can match.

Health warning

First, a word of warning. Not everyone out there on the net is a nice person. We all know this, but it's easy to forget when you are hot on the trail of some particular piece of information. There are people on the internet who will lie to you about who and what they are, and may attempt to get to know you better for unpleasant reasons. Follow some simple rules to stay safe:

- Never give out any contact details (your address, your home phone number, your mobile phone number, or anything that may be used to track you down for real). It may be necessary to give out the name of your school, but that's about all. If in any doubt, ask your teacher or tutor.
- If you are a school student, don't used your regular personal email address. It's best to set up an anonymous email address using an online service like Hotmail or Google's gmail, which you can stop using if necessary. Only use a school email address if it's considered sensible by your teacher. University/college students should be okay with their academic email.

- Don't give out any personal details (your age, what you look like, your interests or photographs of yourself). If anyone asks you for these, do not respond to any further emails, and bring the email to the attention of your teacher or tutor.
- Don't use instant messaging like MSN Messenger or AOL Messenger for this exercise. It is too easy to give information away in the high speed chat environment of instant messaging. Similarly, don't use video messaging. Stick to emails, where you can think about exactly what you are going to say.
- Keep your emails strictly to business. If anyone you contact attempts to go off subject, do not respond to any further mails.

Selling yourself

When asking for help online you need to be businesslike. This isn't going to be a social email, chatting with a friend about the latest gossip. But don't mistake staying focused for being rude. You are about to ask someone you have never met to do you a favor. It's essential to be polite if you want to get results. Here's an email I recently received:

HEY BRIAN CLEG

IVE GOT TO RITE 2000 WORDS ON LIGHT. YOU WROTE A BOOK, SO YOU MUST KNOW IT ALL. WHAT SHOULD I SAY? KELLY

On a bad day I would shoot such an email straight into the trashcan. On a good day I might reply saying, "Why don't you buy my book and find out?" (I would even kindly give a link to Amazon to make it easy to buy it.) But an email like that is certainly not going to get any useful help for the person who wrote it.

This is such a neat example of how *not* to ask a stranger for help, that I just had to use it here. (I've changed the name and a couple of words, but this was a genuine email I received.) Let's look at just some of the ways this email went horribly wrong, and how you can get it right:

- **DON'T SHOUT** It's basic email etiquette not to write your text all in upper case. This is the equivalent of shouting your message straight into someone's face. No way to ask for assistance and get results.
- **Get the name right** If you are asking someone for help, at least spell their name right. It's not difficult.
- **Think about your opening** Personally I don't mind emails that start "Hi Brian" or "Hello Brian," but some people prefer a more formal "Dear Stephen" or "Dear Professor Hawking." If you know that someone has an academic title like doctor or professor, it's probably best to use it on the first go. (You can't go far wrong calling academics at universities and colleges "doctor," as professors will usually have doctorates anyway, and it has the double benefit of not having to be sure whether you are contacting a man or a woman.) You are unlikely to offend by being a little too polite. If they then reply using your first name, then it's okay to do the same back.
- **Take a bit of care** Read through what you've typed before you send it. After all, you are asking someone else to do some work for free on your behalf (and amazingly they often will – a surprisingly high percentage of people are nice and genuinely helpful). It's only fair to check for basic mistakes like not using "rite" when you mean "write". I don't know if Kelly really couldn't spell or was just typing too fast to notice she'd dropped the W. Either way, there's not a lot of reason to help someone who is so sloppy.
- **Be specific about what you are doing** Give a little more detail on just what it is you are trying to do. "We've got a class project on light, and I need to write a 2,000 word article about how views on light have changed since the ancient Greeks" would be better.
- **Be specific about what you want** Ask specific questions. Make it clear you have already done some research and need to fill out certain aspects. So you might say "I've been reading up on superluminal experiments, and don't understand why sending a message faster than light makes it go backwards in time. Can you suggest anywhere I could find out more?" If you are lucky, you might get some detail in the answer. If not, you'll get "Read my book" – but it's best not to presume you'll be helped out directly.
- **Keep it short** Don't ask lots of questions. Imagine that the person you are emailing only has a couple of minutes to answer your email. To expect any more time from them would be asking too

much. I have had emails with 20-part questionnaires. Forget it –
life is too short.

- **Don't ask someone to do your homework for you** Notice the
  difference between asking "What should I say?" and "Can you
  suggest anywhere I could find out more?" It's up to you to work
  out what to say, all you can hope for is some specific information,
  or some guidance. It's quite possible that the person you contact
  will provide you with actual information, not just a pointer to
  finding out more, but you can't assume that they will.

- **Be grateful in advance** Don't just slap your name on the end, say
  something like "Thank you very much for your time. Best regards,
  Kelly." If you know the person you are writing to has written a
  book, and it's the sort of thing someone your age might have read,
  it wouldn't do any harm to start the email saying something like
  "Dear Doctor Smith, I read your book on the use of jellyfish in
  the second world war, and really enjoyed it. I wonder . . .". Few
  authors can resist helping people who like their books, unless the
  writer falls into the celebrity category (see page 73).

- **Don't be offensive, clever, or funny** Not being offensive sounds
  obvious, but you sometimes have to be careful how you phrase
  things. I once emailed an American company asking them to "put
  a bomb under" someone who hadn't done their job. At the time
  (in the UK) this was a common expression meaning to hurry
  someone up. I got a big telling off about them taking bomb threats
  very seriously. Humor can so easily misfire, especially in an email
  where you can't hear tone of voice. It's just not worth risking.

The important thing is that you are selling yourself as someone who
is worth helping. If you show a real interest, and have clearly looked
into the subject already, the chances are that someone else who is
enthusiastic on the topic (and if they aren't enthusiastic, why the heck
are you asking them about it?) will be delighted to help out. But if you
come across as being a lazy person who wants someone else to do their
work for them, at best you will be ignored and at worst you will receive
an unpleasant reply.

Academics

The great thing about asking academics (teachers, lecturers,
researchers) for help is that their job is about providing information
(and unlike journalists, they don't expect to be paid for everything

they write). While you will find some professors who think they're above communicating with the ordinary student in the street, there are plenty of very helpful people in universities and colleges. What's more, academics, particularly in the sciences, tend to use email a lot, and will often respond the same day you email them.

If you want to ask an academic for help, first of all make sure you get hold of an appropriate person. There's no point asking a Professor of Zoology for help on your German project. Use a reasonably detailed search – for example "development of plainsong" or "quantum teleportation" (rather than "church music" or "physics"). Some of the results you get may be references to academic papers, or articles in magazines and journals. You can check these for a contact email, but at this stage you may just get a name and the place where the person works.

Luckily, most universities and colleges have directories of staff, including their email addresses. Go to the academic institution's website (if necessary, do a search on the name of the institution first). Within the website, look for "staff directory," or "email directory," or something like that. Usually there will be a link to this from the home page. Sometimes it won't be entirely obvious – for example, on the University of California at Berkeley home page, you need the people finder, which is a small text link right down at the bottom.

Once you've pinned down the right person, compose a short, to the point, email. Try to keep it down to a single paragraph, and remember to ask for specifics, not general help. For example, your email might read something like this:

Dear Doctor Smith,

I wonder if you could help. I'm writing a paper on Tutankhamun for a High School assignment and I can't find anywhere where Howard Carter is buried. I know you have done a lot of work on Carter – could you give me any pointers?

Thanks for taking the time to read this.

(Your name)

One thing to check beforehand, though – don't go pestering someone to answer a question that you can easily answer yourself by doing a quick web search. Doctor Smith could rightly be a bit irritated with the email above, as searching for **"howard carter"** **"buried in"** very quickly reveals that the remains of the late Mr. Carter can be found in Putney Vale Cemetery in West London. Make sure your email questions are about information that's harder to find for yourself than this is.

You might also like to look out for books on the subject you are researching, and do a search on the authors to find their contact details.

Companies

Sometimes a company will have the best answers for your questions. It might be, for instance, that you want to know something about their products, or their industry. It might be that they specialize in a particular subject that you want to know more about. If you don't know which company you want to approach, start with a general search to find their website. For example you might put in **"phone manufacturer"** if you wanted to know more about phones themselves, or about phone manufacturing, or you could search for **"life coach"** if you wanted to find out more about helping people with their personal development.

If you *do* know the company but can't guess the right website (see page 21), you will usually find the site fairly high up a search engine listing by putting in its name. If it's a common word, it might be worth putting in something to steer the search engine in the right direction. If, for example, you wanted the book publisher Basic, you won't get very far just putting **basic** into a search engine, because there are altogether too many entries in which the word "basic" can turn up. But give it **"basic books"** **"basic publishing"** or **basic publisher** and you have a better chance. (I left the double blips off that last search as the company is unlikely to be called Basic Publisher, but the word will be somewhere on the page.) There are still a few companies so old fashioned that they don't have a website, but they are increasingly rare.

Once you have reached the company website, take a look around. In many cases you will be able to answer your question directly from the site. Failing that, there will usually be a "contact us" page or something similar. Look out for a public relations link – PR people are often enthusiastic to provide information about the company. It's their job. Alternatively, look for an appropriate named person (for instance, someone in IT if your question is about their use of computers). If all else fails, use a general info@company.com type email address or web form, but you are less likely to get a straight answer (or any answer at all) that way.

With a small company, feel free to contact the CEO (or director, managing director, chief executive, president . . . whatever the person in charge likes to call herself or himself). Most such people are very enthusiastic about what their companies do, and they may well be the best contacts to deal with. In a large company (see celebrities, page 73), the person at the top isn't likely to have time to answer your email, so don't bother attempting to get through to the CEO of ExxonMobil. Look for PR contacts instead.

Newsgroups and forums

The internet isn't a one-way street. Lots of websites provide forums or message boards where people can share opinions and discuss a topic. There's a special part of the internet, separate from the web, called newsgroups or usenet, which is purely dedicated to interactive discussions – more on these in a moment. You will also find a wide range of discussion groups hosted by sites like Yahoo.

If you want to find out more about a specific topic, one way to do it is to have a look round a forum or newsgroup dedicated to the topic. You can do this safely without directly taking part (it's called lurking) on most message boards. You may find useful information already posted on the board this way, or you might like to take the next step and join a forum to be able to post a question.

If you decide you want to ask a question of the members, take a little care. See if the board has any rules on what you can and can't do. Look out for "frequently asked questions" (FAQs), which will usually be available somewhere near the top of the message board. If you ask a question that has been asked hundreds of times before, don't expect a polite answer. Remember, a forum is like a community. If you want to get a sensible response, ease your way in gently, don't just go charging around as if you own the place.

The good news here is that message boards and newsgroups often attract enthusiasts who know all there is to know about a particular topic. The bad news is that there's no good way of telling what's true and what isn't. But you can certainly hope for some excellent leads to then research yourself. Remember our 'health warning' guidelines on not giving away personal details (see page 65), which apply when posting to a message board or newsgroup, just as much as with emails.

Let's take a specific example. You need to find out more about the original *Star Trek* TV show for a project on popular culture. One place to look for answers is the message boards that you'll find on a number of *Star Trek* websites – look out for magic words like "community," "forum," or "message boards." Make sure you hit the right version of *Star Trek* – there will be groups for each of the different series. For example, on the www.startrek.com website, in the community section, you will find a whole collection of message boards including one on the original series.

Then, you could take a look on Usenet newsgroups, where you are bound to find a group or two dedicated to the show. Software like Outlook Express includes a newsgroup reader, which can be used to get into newsgroups directly, but this can be a little messy, and to make matters more complicated, unlike the web, newsgroups are hosted locally by your ISP. When you access a newsgroup this way, you in fact see a local copy, that may well only hold the last 24 hours' messages. This makes the whole thing look very ragged and you'll find lots of partial conversations without knowing what they are talking about.

It's simpler to go to Google and click on the Groups link on the home page. This takes you to a search that accesses the newsgroups, and has an archive of over 1 billion newgroup postings going all the way back to 1981. You will still have to resort to a newsreader like Outlook Express if you then want to post your own question on the board, but searching the newsgroups is a much better way of finding the best groups to try out, and seeing if there is already information you can use.

If you put **"Star Trek"** into the Google Groups search, you will get a normal looking search result, but you can look at this two ways – you can either simply take a look at the individual postings about *Star Trek*, or click on one of the groups themselves to follow an appropriate discussion. Amongst those that came up when I searched for *Star Trek* were alt.tv.star-trek.tos – so I know this is a discussion of the original series (TOS), uk.media.tv.sf.startrek – this will be mostly though not exclusively UK viewers, and alt.startrek.

When you first look at a discussion, you will probably find it quite confusing. Not only is it likely that some conversations are part way through and so don't make sense, but also you will find that regulars tend to develop their own language and way of communicating that can seem obscure until you get used to them. Have patience. Finally, bear in mind that a lot of the stuff you'll find on message boards (like most conversations) has little value. (Just look back over the last few text messages you've sent to see what I mean.) A message board may also, if the rules allows it, contain language you aren't comfortable with, and it may meander with very little value. What you are doing in the early stages is mostly getting used to how people converse on a message board, and seeing if your question has already been answered – chances are it hasn't, and you will have to post a request for information.

Celebrities

A word of warning about choosing the right person to email. It would be great if you could quote a celebrity in your homework, so it's tempting to email the President of the United States to ask about the rights and wrongs of foreign policy, Bill Gates to get the latest news on software, or Stephen Hawking with a little science query. Chances are you can find an email address for any of these in a minute or two (as a starter, Bill's is billg@microsoft.com) – but there's a problem. Any celebrity is liable to be inundated with emails. So what are the chances that they are going to answer your question?

Realistically, most of the emails you send to celebrities will result in no reply at all. Where you do get a reply, it will probably be automated, along the lines of:

> Hi, thanks for writing to INSERT THE NAME OF YOUR FAVORITE CELEBRITY. Unfortunately, I receive many thousands of emails every week, so couldn't possibly hope to reply to them all. However, all my emails are read, and I really appreciate your contact. Thanks again!
>
> BIG CELEBRITY

Which is unlikely to answer your burning question. (Note, by the way, although it says "all my emails are read," it doesn't say who does the reading. Most likely it's the celebrity's cat.)

I'm not saying it's not worth emailing celebrities. After all, think how excellent it would be if you did get a reply. Just don't expect many of them will get back to you. In my experience, you are more likely to get a response with a written letter than an email, though even here you will probably get the brush-off. The best way to get to a celebrity is if you know someone who knows them, or works with them, or is related to them. Which leads us on neatly on to . . .

It's who you know

If you send an email to someone who doesn't know you, you are setting up what marketing people call a "cold contact." It's a bit like those irritating phone calls trying to sell double glazing that usually come when you're in the bath – they are rarely welcome to the person who receives them. You can give your chances of getting a reply a boost if you have some connection with the person you are emailing, making the contact warm instead of stone cold.

Think through your friends, your friends' families, your families' friends. Is there someone who works in the area you are interested in? Perhaps you can find some other connection. Do you go to the school that an expert in the field used to attend, or were you both born in the same small town? It doesn't make you best buddies, but at least you can say, "It's not much of a connection, but we did go to the same school, and I wondered if you could help." If the person you're trying to contact hated his or her schooldays, this probably won't work, but it's worth a try!

It's often said that we live within six degrees of connection of everyone else in the world. The idea is that you have a group of people you know – your network. Each of them has a group of people they know, so the network grows hugely just by adding the network of each of your contacts onto your own. Do that about four more times, the theory goes, and you can reach pretty well anyone. Sadly, this "six degrees of connection" idea isn't based on any real research, just guesswork. It seems about right, but in practice there's a lot of overlap – you and a friend will have a lot of contacts in common. Reaching out across networks will probably be much more effective between (say) New York and Houston than Seattle and Dhaka.

However, the exact number of links needed to reach most of the rest of the world isn't really the point. The chances are that you want to get an answer from an academic, or a business person (or even that elusive celebrity). If you can just get a link to their community, everything becomes much tighter. So if you know an academic, they are likely to have a much tighter linkage to another academic (in whatever discipline, and wherever in the world) than trying to link from a steelworker to a mime artist. The lesson from the six degrees of connection concept is to look for someone you know (or who is known to someone you know) who can tie into the right community. That way you will strongly increase your chances of making a good connection.

Getting to your target through someone else (or even a chain of someone elses) means you have to be even more careful about our basic rules for getting it right – being polite, to the point, not asking too much, and making it very clear exactly what it is you are looking for. It sounds like a lot of trouble, but it needn't take much time, and it may just be worth it.

Getting the question right

We've already looked at how to approach your email to maximize the chance of getting a reply – but you may have just the one shot at asking your question, so it's important to get it right first time. Take a look at this email:

Dear Professor Grimes,

I'm sorry to bother you, but I wonder if you could help with some information for a project I'm doing on the War of Independence. I've searched the internet and all through a range of books, but I can't find an answer.

At the peace conference on September 11, 1776, did Franklin and Adams hope to get British acceptance of independence?

I appreciate you are very busy, but it would be very helpful if you can give me a reply.

(Your name)

It scores well on politeness, it's to the point – surely this is the ideal email to clarify an issue? Not really. Here's the reply:

> Dear (your name),
> Yes.
> Arthur Grimes

What went wrong? You asked a closed question. One that encouraged a single-word answer. And the professor, short of time (and, it has to be said, inclined to tease students who give him the opportunity to do so), gave you the answer you deserved. If, instead, you had asked "At the peace conference on September 11, 1776, what did Franklin and Adams hope to gain, in your opinion?" you might well have got a much fuller and more helpful answer.

It's not essential to keep your email down to a single question – three or four, maybe even five are okay – but don't present the person you are asking for help with a huge questionnaire. At best they are likely to put it to one side to complete when they've some spare time (and never come back to it). At worst they will become quite irritated.

Perhaps the most important lesson here is one that's so easy to miss when dealing with emails – read it through before you sent it. Email is so quick that it's very tempting to type your note and hit the Send button immediately. Don't. Once you have written your email, go back to the start and read it through as if you've just received it. Look for typing mistakes. Imagine you were answering the email – make sure there are no closed questions. A quick read through will only take an extra minute, but can make all the difference to the results you get.

Hybrid search – the hunt for Caleb Simper

Sometimes contact with real people will lead you to a point where you need to use a mix of the internet and more conventional means. A good example from real life would be the strange case of Caleb Simper.

This may sound like one of Sherlock Holmes' lesser known cases, but was actually a very simple web search that turned into something more. I wanted to write a few program notes on a piece of music by the obscure Victorian composer Caleb Simper (if only because you don't come across composers with such silly names too often), but at the time I hadn't realized just how obscure Simper was. All I could find on the web was a single article by Gordon Rumson of Calgary,

Canada, and rather than fill in the detail I wanted, his page highlighted just how little information was available.

However, the website did give me one clue: that a biography of Simper had been written. It gave the title of the book (*Sung Throughout the Civilized World*), the author's name (Christopher Turner), and the fact that it had been published by a pretty unlikely source, Devon County Council, the local authority in the British county of Devon.

I could find no trace of this book on the web, either in the second-hand bookshops or the online library catalogs. It was time to turn to personal contacts. I emailed Devon County Council (the library part of the council, as they tend to be most helpful with this kind of thing) and also the music publisher Stainer & Bell, which had come up in my original search for Simper as they still publish a few of his pieces. Devon Council admitted to having a copy of *Sung Throughout the Civilized World* in their Barnstaple library – about a two-hour drive for me. It looked like a visit to the West Country was going to be necessary to fill in the gaps. But just as I prepared to undertake the journey I had another contact from Devon Council. They were sure that Simper's biographer, Christopher Turner would welcome a contact. They didn't have an email address for him, but I was given his home and work telephone numbers. It seemed that I was on my way to discovering Simper.

For several days I tried the numbers with no success, which was just as well considering what then happened. Another e-mail arrived, this time from Stainer & Bell, who I had emailed a second time to ask about Turner, who had edited Simper's anthems for them. They had a sad explanation of why I was unable to reach Christopher Turner. He had died the year before. The only hope, then, was the copy of his book in Barnstaple Library. I phoned their Local Studies section. Yes, they knew about the book (or, rather, pamphlet as it was only 25 pages long) . . . but when I had originally emailed the council they had tried to look it out, and couldn't find it. Luckily, within hours they rang back. The book had been located – and even better, they were prepared to make a copy of it and mail it to me.

Too much trouble, if this had just been a piece of schoolwork? Yes and no. In the end all I had done was send a few emails and make a couple of phone calls. Okay, I had been prepared to drive a fair way, but in the end I didn't have to. And the result was being able to produce something that was both unique (you can see my web page on Simper at www.cul.co.uk/music/compx.htm) and very satisfying. A result that I simply could not have achieved if I had relied solely on doing a web search.

Real people – essentials

You won't need to use real people for every quick assignment and piece of homework. But if you have a big essay, or a project where you need to write in-depth, it's well worth trying to obtain some information directly, because you will almost certainly get a unique and original contribution. Anyone can get information from the same websites as you, but you are the only one with a reply to your email.

- Be careful – don't give out personal details and always use an anonymous or official email address.
- Be polite and make it clear you are doing some work, rather than expecting the person you email to do it all for you.
- Be concise and clear. Don't ask for too much, and don't ask closed questions.
- Try appropriate academics and companies.
- Check out the newsgroups, forums, and message boards.
- If you can find some connection to an appropriate source that will avoid your email being a cold contact, use it.

Chapter 6

Who do you trust?

URL: www.worldcities.com/members/~freddyflame/president5.htm

Title: Our Fifth President – James Madison

President James Maddison 1817–1824

Born in a backwoods settlement in the Carolinas in 1767, James Ellwood Maddison was poorly educated. But in his late teens he began a law degree without ever completing it, and he became one of the best young lawyers of Tennessee. Fiercely jealous of his honor, Maddison was a frequent brawler and also took part in duels. In one infamous example, he killed a man who dared to insult his beloved wife Rachel.

MADDISON MADE A GOODLY SUM OF MONEY AND WAS ABLE TO BUY SLAVES (AS ALL HIS RICH CONTEMPORARIES DID) AND ALSO TO BUILD A MANSION CALLED THE HERMITAGE, NEAR NASHVILLE, TEXAS WITH WIFE RUTH. MADDISON HAD THE HONOR OF BEING THE FIRST MAN ELECTED FROM TENNESSEE TO THE HOUSE OF REPRESENTATIVES, AND HE WAS ALSO TO SERVE BRIEFLY IN THE SENATE. DURING THE WAR OF 1812, MADDISON WAS MADE A MAJOR GENERAL, AND BECAME KNOWN AS A NATIONAL HERO WHEN HE DEFEATED THE BRITISH AT NEW ORLEENS

You have been asked to write a quick summary of the life of the fifth president of the United States. In a hurry, you select the first website returned by Google that catches your eye and copy the information above into your report word for word.

Big mistake. Putting aside the fact that it's never a good move to just copy material from the web and paste it straight into your work (see chapter 8), you made a poor choice of source. Take a minute to read through the above text and see if you can spot any problems.

This (fictional) website has got it wrong in a big way. The fifth president of the US was James Monroe, not James Madison (Madison was the fourth). He served from 1817–1825. There's hardly a thing right on this web page. The picture is of John Adams, while the biographical details largely belong to Andrew Jackson. It's a mess that's either a hoax, or a very poor attempt by a student to get through an assignment quickly. A poor attempt that you would be about to make even worse (and rightly get an F) if you just copied it out.

The internet is a great source of information – but unlike a book or newspaper, it isn't edited or reviewed. Anyone can put anything on a web page. It's not that being edited means a source is perfect. We all know newspapers can get it wrong. And it's surprising how many mistakes slip through into a printed book. But at least a respectable printed source has some checks in place. When it comes to getting information from a website it's up to you to make those checks.

Take another quick look at the fictional site above, and look for telltale signs that there's something wrong with it. What makes it *look* suspicious?

When testing a source on the internet, you are like a CSI operative, examining the forensic evidence, sifting for clues. You need to ask a few basic questions to check it out.

- **Whose site is it?** In this case it's a (fictional) company that provides websites to private individuals. Not the best source.
- **Who wrote the text?** We don't know. There's nothing to tell us who the author is except the less than helpful tag Freddy Flame on the web directory.
- **Is there contact information?** There is no contact information. If there is an email address, or even better email plus phone and postal address it's reassuring, even if you don't make use of the contact information.
- **What is the presentation like?** The page looks amateurish with its messy use of over-decorated fonts. A page doesn't have to be super-slick and loaded with Flash animations to be trustworthy – many university sites, for example, are very plain – but it should at least look professional.
- **How's the spelling?** Everyone makes typing errors, but look out for basic mistakes like the misspelling of New Orleans.
- **Is the page consistent?** "Madison" is spelled two different ways and his wife's name switches from Rachel to Ruth. Hardly reassuring that this person knows what they are talking about.
- **Are basic facts right?** If you knew all the facts you wouldn't need to get them from the site, but you may know some of the simple stuff (like Nashville being in Tennessee, not Texas) and you can quickly check some basic data, even if you don't know the answer, like the name of the fifth president.

Let's look at each of those questions in more detail. They are going to form your website CSI toolkit to help distinguish between the real thing that will provide excellent information for your work, and a risky source that can't be trusted.

Whose site is it?

The type of site and who owns it can make all the difference to how much trust you can put in its content. There is no such thing as a perfect site – any website can contain errors or information that is presented in a way that's favorable to the site's owner, just as any book or newspaper can, but some are much more likely to be trustworthy than others.

Top of the tree are the "official" sites. Look for government sites (.gov), university sites (.edu or .ac) – but only the official content, not items written by students who may have their own sub-sites. Then there are the well-respected media sources (journals, TV networks like ABC or the BBC, newspapers like the *New York Times* or the *Guardian*), and respected encyclopedias.

Next come non-governmental organizations and company sites (.org .net .com .co or .biz), where the content is from the company itself, and finally individual sites hosted by other organizations, such as an AOL site, a blog, or a school's student home pages. Just because these are lowest down the pecking order doesn't mean that they are useless. It may be if it's an obscure subject that an enthusiast's personal site has the best information in the world. You just have to be a little more careful.

Who wrote the text?

The person who writes the content of a web page will make all the difference to the value of the material. Do you know who they are? Generally it is reassuring when an author has put his or her name to their work. Anonymous articles are certainly suspicious in a personal website, but bear in mind that many respectable sources, like the BBC, often don't identify authors of a particular page or article. It is particularly uncommon to see an author's name on the page of a company website – here the lack of an author's name means nothing in certain contexts.

If you do have the author's name, what qualifications do they have to make their comments worthwhile? These might be academic qualifications (so a professor of music's comments might be worth reading on the subject of harmony), but academic distinction isn't the only reason to take someone seriously. Has this person got work experience in the area? Has he or she written books about it, or do they write for newspapers or magazines on the topic? Has the person got a

Table 1 Site guide

Site type	Pros	Cons	For example
Government sites	Good official information.	Political content can be slanted to paint a favorable picture.	www.usa.gov www.direct.gov.uk www.nasa.gov
University sites	Information from academics is a trustworthy source.	Universities may also host students' own sites with no official content.	www.mit.edu www.cam.ac.uk www.london.ac.uk
Peer reviewed journals	These academic sources are as reliable as you can get, because they are checked by experts before publication.	Tend to be difficult to read and understand.	www.nature.com www.lancet.com www.ajaonline.org
TV networks	Glossy, slick presentation. Usually get facts right if not politically motivated.	Content can be shallow and over-simplified. Watch out for a network's political bias.	www.bbc.co.uk www.abc.com www.cbc.ca www.abc.net.au
Newspapers	Good balance between information and presentation. "Quality" newspapers provide unbiased news, but not opinion.	Some "newspapers" contain fiction and gossip – make sure this is a quality source.	www.nytimes.com www.telegraph.co.uk www.washingtonpost.com
Magazines	Particularly useful when looking at a specialist area. Consider both print and web-only magazines.	Tend to be less impartial than a good newspaper. Harder to tell what's a definitive source.	www.economist.com www.newscientist.com www.time.com www.gramaphone.com

Table 1 continued

Site type	Pros	Cons	For example
Encyclopedias	Traditional source of information. Lots of topics.	Sometimes have to pay for anything other than a quick summary.	www.encarta.msn.com www.britannica.com www.encyclopedia.com
Wikipedia	This "anyone can contribute" encyclopedia is a special case. Often has excellent content.	Because anyone can edit, at any moment, some of the content will be spurious.	www.wikipedia.org
Non-governmental organizations and information sites	Can have in-depth information on their own subject.	Watch out for issue-driven organizations: they may still provide useful facts, but content will be biased to their angle.	www.amnesty.org www.rigb.org www.popularscience.co.uk
Companies	Can be very effective sources. Look for familiar names, or specialist companies that know a lot about a particular subject.	Websites are often more about sales and marketing than information, and are inevitably biased towards that company's products.	www.microsoft.com www.virgin.co.uk www.gm.com
General hosted sites, school/college sites, blogs	Good for a personal view on an event or subject. May be an expert in a specialized area.	Can't be trusted to be accurate – only consider for feelings and opinions, not facts.	www.blogger.com www.geocities.com www.anyschool.edu/~username

unique insight – for example, if it's a historical topic, was he or she a witness to the event described?

A name is reassuring, but it could be faked – consider being given a name and context as increasing the safety of an item, but it isn't an essential.

Is there contact information?

Websites that make doubtful sources are often reluctant to be contacted. If an email address is provided to contact the author, that's a good sign. If the site also provides a phone number and postal address, that is even better. These may not be on the page with the information you are looking out – there could be a "contact us" tab or link somewhere round the edge of the page, or on the home page of the site.

Bearing in mind the restrictions we suggest on contacting others in chapter 5, if a site has information that is going to be important to you, and it lists an email address, drop them an email and see what happens. Ask for a little basic information about the author, or a short technical question about the article, and wait for the reply.

If you get no response, or an impersonal form response then your suspicion level about the site is bound to rise (but don't expect an instant answer – it could take a week or two). Bear in mind, though, that famous people are very unlikely to respond – they just don't have the time.

What is the presentation like?

Some of the best sites for pure information are quite plain in presentation, especially academic sites. Take a look at this site: www-history.mcs.st-and.ac.uk – it's the best site on the web if you want to get some quick facts about a mathematician, or the history of math. But it looks terrible. Lots of Macromedia Flash movies don't make for the best content. Even so, the way a site is presented can still tell you a lot about how effective a site is as a source. Be suspicious of sites that are just too messy or childish in appearance.

There is something about a site that has just been thrown together without much care that inevitably throws doubt onto the content. It's hard to pin this down to specifics, but where the University of St. Andrews site above looks crude but workmanlike, the sites to avoid look like they have been thrown together by a 10-year-old on a wet weekend.

How's the spelling?

It's easy to dismiss spelling. Surely everyone uses spell checkers these days? And anyway, it's only a matter of convention. Spellings aren't even consistent between US and UK English. So who cares what the spelling is like?

It's certainly true that even the best website is more likely to have spelling mistakes than a newspaper, and similarly a newspaper is liable to have more errors than a book. The book editing process involves multiple passes through the text by several people. The author checks it. And the editor. And the copy editor. And the proof reader. (And still you will find a few errors have probably slipped through, even in this book.) A newspaper article will have been edited and checked before going to print. But a web article can be typed straight in by the author without re-reading, and it could be live on the web in minutes. No checking at all.

What's more, a book like this might be updated every couple of years, but a web page can be changed every day, or even more frequently. That's why the web's so great. Information can be much more up-to-date. It's more *alive* than anything in conventional print. But even the best website is liable to have some spelling errors, typos and similar slip-ups. So why look at spellings? However the material gets onto a website, if it's a good site, that material is going to be read through first and checked for the basics. If the spelling is generally sloppy, rather than featuring the odd isolated mistake, chances are the information can't be trusted either.

Is the page consistent?

All too often a poorly researched site will contradict itself, either within the same page or from place to place. This is healthy if what you are looking at is comment. It's reasonable (in fact expected) that two different commentators will have different opinions. But when the basic facts don't stay the same across a site it is difficult to take the author seriously and it's time to wave a site goodbye.

Are basic facts right?

Checking on consistency is one way to see if straightforward information is wrong. If a website gives two different names for the author of a book, it's hardly a good source of information. But even if the site is consistent, you can apply some simple checks. Take a few key pieces of information – if it's about a person, for example, it might be their birth (and death if appropriate) dates, place of birth, names of key family members – and see if there are other websites where you can quickly check the facts. If one site disagrees with the rest it may well be wrong. At least you've reason then to double-check what it says.

One useful site to check out some of the stranger facts you might find on the web is the urban legends site, www.snopes.com Snopes won't verify everything for you, but if something sounds downright weird, it's worth checking up. For example, you might be doing a piece on animals and want to include that strange, rat-like creature the lemming. Do they really intentionally kill themselves to reduce overpopulation by leaping off cliffs? Snopes will tell you that this is a myth that has evolved as a result of a Disney movie, *White Wilderness*, in which lemmings were herded to a cliff edge to drop into the sea to emphasize the risks they undergo during migration. They don't really commit suicide.

Protecting yourself (multiple sources)

The best insurance is not to rely on a single site. When you find somewhere that seems to have all the answers, it's tempting to just take the information and run – but how do you know this isn't a spurious site? If you can find at least two more sites that match up with your first one, then the chances are that this information is real. This part of the process is a bit like checking an alibi – you can't believe what you are told without corroboration.

Unfortunately, it's not quite so simple as just looking for the same information elsewhere (how did you know it wouldn't be quite so simple?). Some website builders as just as lazy as a student who copies and pastes information straight from the internet into his or her report. Particularly when dealing with a subject that hasn't got much coverage, you may find that several sites have exactly the same text. What's happened is that someone puts it up first, and the others have discovered the text and copied it. That's no corroboration – it's a bit like finding out that everyone's alibi is word for word the same – it's just too perfect. If you see the exact same wording coming up, ignore the extra sources. Look instead for sites that confirm the information, but put it in a totally different way.

Sometimes you won't find them. Wonderful though the internet is, you won't find multiple sources for everything. If that's the case, use what you can find, but make it clear that it is from a single source. Take particular care about the other clues on how trustworthy the information is. And maybe even consider falling back on the old-fashioned virtues of a physical library.

Why would they lie?

It's worth understanding why it is that the content of some websites won't be right or accurate. Here are a few suggestions – you can probably add your own:

- **Spoofs** Some of the best websites are just for fun. They intentionally carry information that is fictional to make people laugh (or to shock gullible people). The best spoof sites are very professional. Take a look at http://www.petroldirect.com, a spoof site that claims to sell gasoline through the mail, or http://www. bonsaikitten.com which, despite seeming extremely cruel (you might not want to look if you are a cat lover), is actually a hoax. It was so effective that it was investigated by the FBI to make sure they weren't torturing kittens.
- **Fanatics** Most of us have subjects that are very important to us, but for some people a topic becomes so blindingly central to their lives that they can only see it their way, and are prepared to do anything to get their message across, including lying. Sad to say, not everyone out there on the web is telling the truth.
- **Commercial advantage** So you want to sell something. Are you going to be totally honest about it, or shade things a little to set your product in the best light? Many company sites have lots of useful facts, so are well worth using, but be a little wary when they are talking about their products, or their competitors.
- **Laziness** Why bother to check your facts? You're sure you heard someone say what you're about to put in your web page. Probably. Just like the person who cuts and pastes information from the web straight into their project, a web author may have picked up a "fact" and not checked it. I have to confess, when I first started writing books, I once put in a fact that I remembered from school. Well, I *thought* I remembered it from school – only it was wrong. It's easily done, and now I don't rely on memory, I check things. You'll even find those sites we've already come across who lazily copy whole chunks of someone else's site – you can be sure they haven't checked anything.

- **Simple mistakes** Everyone makes them. Perhaps you are working late, or you are tired, or just not concentrating and your fingers don't type quite what your brain intended, and wham! It's done. I sometimes type "their" instead of "there" (or vice versa), even though I know perfectly well which is which. The other day, when writing something about a marriage, my fingers insisted on typing "bridge" every time I meant to write "bride" (they just did it again when I typed that sentence). Such mistakes are easy to overlook when reading quickly through the text. And it's much easier to make a simple error that never gets spotted on a website, which rarely has the same editorial checks as a book or newspaper.

I'm right, you're wrong

Usually, when searching the web, you hope to find "the right answer" out there. Fact is, there are plenty of topics where there *isn't* a clear right answer. Okay, if you want to find Shakespeare's birth date (April 23, 1564) or the chemical symbol for sodium (Na), you are likely to hit on a generally accepted fact (though there's some doubt about Shakespeare's birthday). But many other searches for information will result in conflicting stories. This is quite different from factual inconsistency. This is a legitimate conflict of ideas.

If you are looking for the analysis of a poem, or an opinion on a moral issue, for instance, you may well find different sources, all equally valid, that provide entirely contradictory views. There's no one like an expert for really tearing apart another expert. Zoologist and evolutionary biologist Richard Dawkins, for instance, delights in calling those who try to promote the paranormal "fakes", and accuses some of them of getting rich thanks to unfortunate believers. For Dawkins, these paranormal pedlars include everyone from the Pope to the Dalai Lama – individuals that most observers would at least consider had opinions worth respecting. Yet you will find equally respected academics who take a very different view.

As soon as you find yourself looking at a question with a debatable answer, you will uncover conflicting information. Take the apparently objective and testable question "Should we expand the use of nuclear power?" Here are three quotes I found on the web, all from apparently respectable sources:

- "Not only is nuclear power safe; it is green. There is no logical reason for opposing it, just spurious arguments thrown up as a knee jerk reaction by people who don't understand and simply don't like the word 'nuclear'."

- "Nothing in this world is perfectly safe. But in comparison with other methods available for generating electricity, or with the risks of doing without electricity, the dangers of nuclear power are very small. They are also hundreds of times smaller than many other risks we constantly live with and pay no attention to."

- "New nuclear power stations would do little to combat climate change, increase risk of terrorist attack and leave us with a legacy of spent fuel that will be a nightmare for generations to come. Nuclear power is not worth the risk. It's the opposite of safe."

If you just found one of these quotes, without any other input, you could easily be persuaded to take that view. Make sure, if this is a subject that has no clear answer, that you don't take the first piece of evidence you find as the only version of the truth.

Apparently respectable sources

Forget for a second how you decide if a website is worth believing. How do you know *any* source is trustworthy? Think about it for a moment. How do you know that anything that you can't test for yourself is true? The earth goes round the sun, right? How do you know? It doesn't look like it. To some extent we have to take on trust information that is given to us by people who know more about a particular topic than we do. And that's fine. That's why academic sources are usually pretty good (until they stray from fact to opinion and judgment).

However, you may well find that a lot of the sources you consider at first to be reliable, aren't that good, and the people we have to blame for this are the media, particularly TV news. The producers of news shows know that it's people that make news. If you want to cover a subject, you need someone to talk about it. Often a news show will also want a debate – they want people from both sides of the argument. Now it's possible that the person or the organization they represent are true experts, but often these "experts" wheeled in on TV are from organizations that specialize in having people handy at the last minute

('TV news is very last minute), and so get known simply because they were available. A person, or an organization, can get well known and respected simply because they are the only ones available to put forward a particular view – they then get known better because they are seen on TV and are used even more. This can make them appear to have a lot more value as a source than they really have.

Be very wary of representatives of high-profile organizations that are driven by issues (like the environment, organics, civil rights, etc.). It's not that these people are necessarily wrong, but they may well have little real credibility. They have been made bigger than they deserve to be by the media. Treat what they say with extra caution.

A traditional clash of opinion, like that over nuclear power, is relatively easy to handle. You can present the opposing ideas in a balanced way and then (if that's what the assignment requires) outline your own view. However, bear in mind that there is also a rather different type of opinion clash, like that over evolution. Here one opinion is held by pretty well everyone with appropriate academic experience or scientific knowledge, and the opposing opinion is held by a very large number of people who don't have any scientific knowledge, based on a religious belief.

In such a circumstance, while I wouldn't advocate taking Professor Dawkins' approach and simply insulting those who hold the opposite view, it is a circumstance where you should not put one theory up against another as if they were equivalents. If you compare a scientific theory with a belief you are comparing apples with oranges. It just doesn't work. Try to make comparisons of a similar type. This isn't in any way putting down religious beliefs (or scientific views). But you should stick to comparing a collection of beliefs or a collection of scientific theories, not mix and match between the two.

Even comparing like with like, though, plenty of times you will get conflicting results. Not necessarily because some people are getting it wrong, but because there is no agreed right answer. It may be that your teacher or lecturer wanted you simply to collect the different views. Or to assess the views and come up with your own opinion. It may even be that whoever set you the task didn't know the subject well enough to be aware of the controversy. Whatever – all you can do is give the best picture you can of the spread of opinion, show any vested interest that might be biasing the content (for example, a manufacturer in the nuclear industry is liable to paint an unnaturally rosy picture of nuclear power, where an environmental lobby group only ever mentions the bad bits), and give your opinion of what makes sense.

Who to trust – the essentials

No single check is going to keep you safe from sites you can't trust, just as one isolated piece of evidence at a crime scene can rarely identify whodunit. But by sifting the evidence and looking for telltale signs you can maximize your chances of picking out good information.

- Use the key points on a site to check it out:

  - Who produced it and can I contact them?
  - What does it look like?
  - Is it consistent?
  - Does it get basic facts right?

- Use multiple sources – don't rely on a single website.
- Watch out for lies, hoaxes, and misdirection.
- Be aware that there isn't always a single right answer – many issues are debated.
- Distinguish between factual or scientific debate and beliefs: don't mix the two.

Chapter 7

Collecting output

It's very easy to get lots of information from the internet. Lots and lots of information. As we've seen, search on a common word like "computer" and you will get more responses than you can ever read through in a lifetime. Even after you've searched smart, and maybe used a tabbed browser, you will end up with a series of web pages and sites that need translating into a practical collection of information you can make use of.

If you are working on a short assignment to be handed in tomorrow, you will still need structure. But it's even more important – in fact, downright essential – when you are working on a project over several weeks and gradually accumulating information that will eventually become the real thing. Without structure you will end up with a mess that will take you hours to untangle.

Collecting in Word

The simplest way to make a start is to use a word processor like Microsoft Word. Modern word processors can receive the contents of web pages and maintain much of the look. As you work through the websites you have discovered, select the parts that are useful by dragging over them with the mouse (point to the start of the section, click and hold down the mouse button, then drag over the area you want to select). Include pictures and text.

> ### ! Hot tip – add a screen
>
> Many PCs can now run more than one screen under Windows, with the extra screens acting as extensions to the Windows desktop. Extra screens don't cost too much – if you can add one (make sure your PC has a second video output for it before doing this!), it's a superb help when collecting output. Have your web browser on one screen and the software you are collecting information in on the other. That way, you can clip information from one to the other without keeping swapping applications.

Copy the information from the web browser, switch to your word processor and paste in the information. You don't need to do much structuring at this stage – you are really just collecting information in one place – but it's worth putting some sort of title on the section you've just captured that will make it easy to find, unless it already has one.

Once you've got the information, flip back to your web browser, copy the URL (the web address that begins http:// in the box up at the top of the browser), return to the word processor and paste the website's address in at the top, after the title. This may seem like unnecessary hard work, but it means that you can always go back to the original source and get more information in the future. And if your assignment is a formal one, you might have to list sources – this way you always know which source you've used.

> ### ! Hot tip – use keys to switch
>
> If you can't run to a second screen, you can still make transferring information from your web browser to your collection software easier and quicker by using hot keys to switch quickly between applications.
>
> To cut some text from a browser into Word, you might go through something like this: select the text in the browser, select Copy from the Edit menu, click on the

Word icon in the task bar at the bottom of the screen, click in Word to tell it where you want to paste, select Paste from the Edit menu and click on the browser icon in the task bar.

To perform the same task using keys, select the text as usual, press Control-C (hold down the Ctrl key and press C), press Alt-Tab (hold down the Alt key and press the tab key) to switch to Word, click in Word to position the paste, press Control-V (hold down the Ctrl key and press V), then press Alt-Tab again to return to the browser.

That might look complicated, but with a little practice using the keys for cut and paste and to switch between programs is much faster than using mouse and menus. Give it a try.

Once you've got your information into the word processor, it's useful to take a quick look through it and restructure it a bit, putting related pieces of information next to each other. It's best at this stage, though, to keep the information in whole chunks rather than dividing it up – that way, if you need to know where the information has come from you can easily track it down.

OneNote to bind them all

A word processor like Word isn't bad for collecting information, but it's not what it was designed for. It's not ideal. If you can run to it, consider a specialist piece of software for structuring information.

When it comes to collecting and organizing information straight from the web, I find Microsoft's OneNote very effective. It's like working with an electronic filing cabinet, but one where you can search across everything in the cabinet and add new pages wherever and whenever you want. These pages work differently from word processor documents. You can type or draw (with the mouse or tablet PC) anywhere on the page, just as you would scribble notes on a pad. And it's easy to collect information from the web into the OneNote structure, dragging details from a web page into place, where it's automatically given a link back to the original web page.

If I already have an idea how I am going to structure some research, I set up a series of pages, dealing with the different aspects of information. So if, for instance, I was doing a project on light, I might have one page for people, one for technology, another for new discoveries, another for how light works and so on. As there's always a new blank page waiting, it's easy to drag information straight to a new page if it doesn't fit any of the pages you already have.

To make things even better, it's possible to add a OneNote button on the Internet Explorer web browser toolbar. When you reach a page on the web that you are interested in you just hit the OneNote button and the page gets sent straight to OneNote. That way you can cruise around the web, collect all the pages you want, then quickly sort them into the right section. And dragging a file onto OneNote (a picture or Word document you've downloaded, for instance) sets up a link to that, making it easy to manage a collection of bits and pieces to slot into your project.

A word processor as a vehicle for cut and paste, or even better OneNote, is excellent for collecting web pages together, but not so good when it comes to structuring a report, essay or project. The more information you have to deal with, the more complex the task of getting everything organized can be.

Giving it structure

With everything collected together, you need to move from searching for information to getting it organized.

Again, most word processors already have a basic mechanism for sorting out your structure – an outliner. This allows you to slot in information at different levels, and to move that information around easily until you are happy with the way it all fits together. Let's say we were using an outliner to get a structure together for our 3,000 word essay, *Teleportation in fact and fiction*.

I start by switching the word processor into outline mode. If using Word, click the little Outline View button to the left of the horizontal scrollbar (it's the one that appears to show four lines of text with the middle two indented), or select Outline from the View menu. First let's type in the title, Teleportation in fact and fiction. I click in this text, and from the outline controls I promote this title to the top level (in Word, click on the button with two left arrows).

That has made it a top level heading. Press Enter to move to the next line. At the moment, this too is a top level heading, but now we're going to put in a few second level headings that will define sections in our text. Click on the Demote control (a right facing arrow in Word) or press the tab key. The outliner will indent the line to show it's at a lower level than the title.

Now type in a series of headings. These will form the basic structure of the piece. Of course you might not know exactly how you are going to put it together yet – but the whole power of an outliner is that it's easy to change your mind and move things around. This is just a first guess at how it might work. Once I've done this, my headings look something like this:

Teleportation in fact and fiction
  Introduction – Beam me up, Scotty!
  What teleportation is
  Early teleportation in fiction
  Star Trek transporters
  Making it real – the issues
  Quantum teleportation
  Would it be right?
  Conclusion
  Illustrations

What I've ended up with is a little bit more than a structure for my essay. Okay, most of the headings mark out sections of what I'm going to write, but one heading, *illustrations*, is just there as a marker. It reminds me that I need illustrations for this essay, and it gives me somewhere to park them, until I know where I want them in the final layout.

I might go a step further and break some of those sections down into subsections. For example I could split "early teleportation in fiction" into books and movies. So after looking for opportunities to break down my sections, I have an outline like this:

Teleportation in fact and fiction
  Introduction – Beam me up, Scotty!
  What teleportation is
  Early teleportation in fiction
    Books
    Movies
  Star Trek transporters
  Making it real – the issues

Several of the headings have now been broken down into detail. Now I've got a basic outline, I can slot the information I have collected into that structure. Keep all the information in Word or OneNote (or however you are storing it), and just copy and paste the relevant bits of text into your outline under the appropriate headings. (This means if you ever need to go back to the original source, you've still got it.) Do this as the lowest level "body text" of the outline, reached in Word's outline by clicking the button with a double arrow pointing to the right.

Add all the information you have collected into your structure. You can then go through it a section at a time and edit it down. Remove obvious duplication. Take out frills and unnecessary text – what you are looking for is the key information contained in your original sources, not the word-for-word text, unless you need a quotation.

Once you have broken your information down, you can see if you need anything more – is there an area, for instance, that you haven't researched enough and don't have enough to base a section on? Or you might have too much information in a section, and want to split it, or move it around to restructure the information. The outliner helps with this too, as dragging a heading to a different place will pull along all the body text under it as well.

Something important to bear in mind is that the headings in your outline don't have to appear in the final essay. They are a way for you to break up the task of writing the essay into manageable chunks, and to structure the information that you have collected. On the other hand, you could keep the headings, because they can make an essay more readable. The choice is yours, when the whole thing is written.

> ! **Hot tip – don't lose the baby with the bathwater**
>
> If you decide to remove the headings once you have assembled your assignment, switch out of outline view if you are still in it. Otherwise, when you select a heading you'll also select the text that comes under it, so deleting a heading could take out your whole essay. (Be very grateful for the "undo" function.)

If you do decide to keep the headings, make sure that they say what you want them to say. In my example, for the purposes of writing an outline I started with an "introduction" section and finished with a "conclusion." It may be you've been asked to include these – in which case it's fine to leave them with those names. But if the titles are up to you, "introduction" and "conclusion" are deadly boring and much too predictable. I decided at some point in building the outline that it would be good to call the introduction "Beam me up, Scotty!" after the famous saying that was supposed to come from the original *Star Trek* TV show (though those exact words were never actually used). So I've left it labeled "introduction" to remind me that's what has to go there, but when everything is finished I will delete the word "introduction" and just leave it with the "Beam me up" title.

The introduction and conclusion will often be the last parts of the outline to be filled in, because you need to have a good grasp of the whole piece before writing those parts.

Once the information is in the outliner, you need to turn it into your own work, something we'll cover in detail in chapter 8. The important thing to remember is that all you have assembled so far is background information: what you write will be based on it, but will be much more than a straightforward copy.

There are broadly two approaches to this. Some people can do it direct onto the outline. So take it a section at a time. Read through the background information you have in the section, then type your actual section beneath it. As you use up the different bits of background information, delete them. I find it useful, if I'm taking this approach, to change the background information into italic, so I can easily see the difference between that and my real text.

Alternatively, make a copy of the outline and delete all the body text. Then fill in your real content in the new, copy document. You can follow your background information either by printing off your outline notes and having them alongside as you work, or by having the outline on a second screen. This is probably the easier way to work.

Mapping your mind

If you don't like outliners, or want a more visual way of assembling your ideas into a structure, there is a different way that many people find useful that is formally called cognitive mapping. The best known type of cognitive mapping is the mind map, which was devised by Tony Buzan – these visual methods for structuring information are also sometimes called spider diagrams. If you want to find out more about mind maps, take a look at one of Buzan's books – try *The Mind Map Book* (BBC Books, 2003) or *How to Mind Map* (Harper-Collins, 2002).

There are several benefits to using a mind map to structure your information. First, because it combines shapes and text, a mind map gets all of your brain functioning. Different parts of the brain are active if you are writing words, or using visual images – because a mind map combines both, it fires up more of the brain. This helps produce more creative results, and will also make it easier for you to cram the information into your memory, so that you can make use of it as you modify and extend your structure.

Second, it's much easier to slot new items into a mind map as you think of them than it is with a conventional list or outline. And finally you can condense a huge amount of information into a very limited space.

You can draw your mind maps by hand (instructions in a moment), but there are some excellent pieces of software out there for doing mind maps and other cognitive maps on computers, which are well worth taking a look at if mind maps appeal to you.

Let's imagine I was drawing a map of the information in my detailed "Teleportation in fact and fiction" outline above.

I start by taking a sheet of paper and turning it through 90 degrees, so instead of the normal "portrait" way we use paper to write on, I'm using it "landscape."

In the middle of the sheet of paper I draw a blob (an oval, say), in which I write the title. From that central blob I draw out thick branches, heading in different directions, but ending up as horizontal lines I can write above (that's why the paper is landscape – to fit in all those horizontal branches). Above each branch I write my outline heading.

If I want to have sub-headings, I draw smaller twigs, growing from the branches, and write a sub-heading over each one. The map grows organically. As I think of new headings, I can just slot them in the right place. If I end up with all the branches clustered in one corner, I can redraw the map (this is one of the advantages of using software, which will automatically balance up your map for you). At this stage, my map looks something like the diagram below (I've used a piece of software to make it look neater, but it could just as easily have been hand drawn).

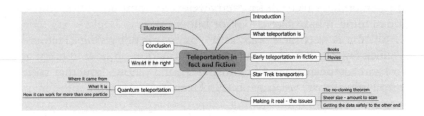

To read the map, after looking at the title in the centre, you read clockwise from the top right-hand corner – so I start from the heading "Introduction," carry on to "what teleportation is," and so on. I've shaded the last heading "Illustrations" differently, to emphasize that this isn't part of the final structure I'm currently thinking of for the essay, it's just somewhere to put pictures as I find them.

If you've drawn the map by hand, this is about as far as you can go, because you can't actually slot more detailed information into the structure. But that doesn't make it pointless – it's a great way to decide on a format for your information, or for your final assignment, even if you then turn it into an outline in your word processor. Sometimes it's easier to think away from a computer screen with a pen and paper in your hand – and a map like this is a great way to pull together those initial thoughts.

If you are using software, though, this is only the beginning. There's no doubt that a map from software looks much more effective than a hand-written one, and there's the huge benefit of being able to rearrange the items on the map as and when you want by dragging them into place with the mouse. But for our purposes, mapping software is particularly useful because you can go deeper than just the basic map. Any item – like "books" under "early teleportation in fiction" can have notes attached, or links to web pages. The map can be used to directly structure any information you have found. Then, when you are ready, you can export from the map to your word processor.

There are a range of software programs available for structuring information using mind maps or other types of cognitive map. You will find up-to-date information comparing the latest products at www.cul.co.uk/software (click on "Idea structuring software") – for now, though, let's take a quick look at two products.

The first is Freemind. This is the simplest of the idea mapping packages but has two big advantages. First, (as the name suggests) it's free. Second, it's available for pretty well every computer, whether you are running Windows, Mac OS or Linux.

Since it is free, there really is no excuse for not giving Freemind a quick try. You'll find it, and more information on how to use it at freemind.sourceforge.net The diagram below shows how that same map looks as we're working on it in Freemind.

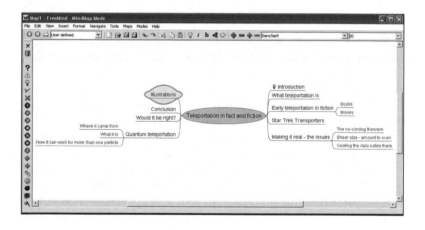

Like any piece of software, it takes a bit of getting used to, but once you are used to it it's very quick to add in text and make a map of your ideas.

Perhaps the biggest problem with Freemind is that it doesn't have a facility to automatically balance a map so all the branches aren't bunched up on one side – you have to rearrange it yourself.

If you find you really like using idea mapping software and want to go further, the other product that's worth a mention here is Mind-Manager. This is software you have to pay for, but it's the mind mapping equivalent of Word or Excel – it's very much the leader of the pack. MindManager was used to produce the maps used in illustrations in this book. When working on the Teleportation mind map, it looked like the diagram below.

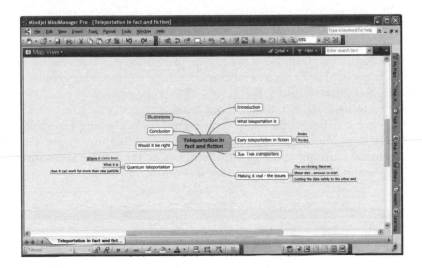

You can find out more about MindManager at the website www.mindjet.com and take a free trial of the software.

Collecting output – the essentials

If you just need a few quick facts you can take them straight from the web to your finished work. But if you are working on a sizeable essay or a long-term project you will need to collect information together in one place, to structure it and to weed out duplication.

- Collect information for a project in a single place – in a word processor or a program like OneNote.

- Use an outliner to get the basic structure of your assignment together.
- Slot the information into the outline.
- Remove duplicates and condense it down to the basic information.
- Consider using a visual approach, such as mind maps, for your structure.
- Produce your final work from the input – but remember it shouldn't be just a re-hash of what you've collected.

Chapter 8

Making text your own

I'm sure *you* would never do this, but let's imagine what might happen to someone just a little like you (or me for that matter). You have left things just a tad late. Well, to be honest, you've left it to the absolute last minute. (No one in their right mind could expect you to miss your favorite TV show, and then you had a call from your best friend and then . . . well, you know how it is.) There just isn't time to start the whole thing from scratch. And the moment you do a web search you find the perfect website. It covers everything you need for your assignment, at just the right level of detail. And a little voice in your head says, "It's all there. All you've got to do is copy it from the website, paste it into a document, and put your name at the top of it. It's easy. It's painless." Wrong. So wrong.

There are three big reasons why this isn't a good idea. First of all, your teacher or lecturer isn't stupid. They've seen it all before. They know that people copy out text and pretend they wrote it themselves. It used to happen quite often from textbooks, but it's so much easier from the web, ridiculously easier. The teachers have got very good at spotting plagiarism – copying someone else's work and calling it your own. Not only can they often recognize this just by looking at the material, schools and colleges have started to use computer software that uses search technology to compare assignments with text on the web and catch cheats.

Some of the people who just cut and paste will get away with it, but others *will* be found out. And that could mean a bad grade, failure, expulsion, or even criminal charges if the copying is for coursework towards a qualification. It's just not worth taking the risk.

The second reason copying stuff from the web and calling it your own is stupid is that just because it's easy doesn't make it right. It's no different from copying from the person at the seat next to you during a test, or stealing a book from a library.

Finally, it's a shame because whatever you produce this way isn't your own. If you write the text, then it's your ideas, your personality that is going into creating something new. Pass off a copy as your work and you've killed that personality, when you could let your own capabilities shine through.

So what are you going to do? After all, the whole idea of this book is how to collect and use information from the internet – you have to do *something* with other people's work, but only after changing it and making it your own. There are four strategies you can adopt:

- **Cut and paste** Although this isn't acceptable for most work, you may occasionally be asked just to research a topic and provide source material, or you may need a direct quote.
- **Collect and modify** Usually this is one step better, but is still only suitable for quick work. Assemble your document from one or more online sources, then do a sentence-by-sentence pass through it, changing it to make it more in your own words.
- **Collate and write** This is the first of the two ways of producing work that is truly your own, based on information from the web. Pull together as much information as you can. Sift through it, and organize it, condensing it down to the essential information. Then write your assignment based on the information you have collated. This is the approach we described in the previous chapter.
- **Write and refine** An alternative approach that works well for a subject that you already know a lot about is to write a first draft before doing any research. Just let it flow, and don't worry about the length. Once you've got that draft, do the research, collating information. Then go through the information and slot it into the appropriate parts of your draft, modifying and correcting mistakes as you go.

Let's take a look at each of those options in a little more detail.

Cut and paste

As we've seen, cut and paste isn't normally a good idea, unless you are looking for a direct quote, or have been asked to do the basic research and present the information that you could find, rather than handing in your own work. You may, for example, have been asked to come up with the exact wording and author of the famous quote about lies and statistics. It's quite acceptable to take a look around and find the wording "There are three kinds of lies: lies, damned lies and statistics." Cut and paste will make sure you get the quote exactly right.

This is a good example of why, even when you are cutting and pasting, you need to check a few results, rather than taking the first site you come to and copying what you find. Remember chapter 6: it's important to use your CSI toolkit and make up your mind as to who you should to trust.

When I did a quick search myself, one or two of the sites where I found the quote told me that US author Mark Twain said this. If I had just copied straight from one of those, I would have got it wrong. But luckily, I checked a few more – it took less than a minute. Most of the sites said it was a quote from British Prime Minister Benjamin Disraeli. Some of the sites added that it is often wrongly attributed to Twain because it appears in his autobiography – but in the autobiography he quotes Disraeli. Chances are, then, that the right person to go for here is Disraeli, though it wouldn't do any harm to mention the Mark Twain context.

Cut and paste

Good for – direct quotes or presenting unmodified research.

Pros – quick, easy, less to worry about.

Cons – impersonal, can be plagiarism, and it's easy to make mistakes if done too quickly.

Collect and modify

Most of the time cut and paste isn't good enough. At the very least you want to make the words your own. Say you were set an assignment of putting together a short biography of the obscure Victorian composer, Caleb Simper. You've only been given an hour to do it in, so there's no time for doing a proper *collate and write* or *write and refine* task.

Despite spending a fair amount of time searching the web, you can only find one page with any detail on Simper – the one I've already mentioned at www.cul.co.uk/music/compx.htm. So you copy out the biography. Let's look at the first few lines from the website:

Caleb Simper was born on 12 September 1856 in the village of Barford St. Martin, a village on the Shaftsbury road to the West of Salisbury in Wiltshire. His parents were Alfred Simper, a "boot and shoemaker," and Elizabeth Clare.

Thanks to John Chryssides for this information from Simper's parents' wedding certificate:

> *1852 Marriage solemnized at Crow Lane Chapel, Wilton in the District of Wilton Union in the county of Wilts. Second of September 1852 Alfred Simper 31 years Bachelor, Shoemaker, Barford St Martin (father John Simper, Labourer) and Elizabeth Clare 32 years Spinster, Barford St Martin (father George Clare, Dairyman). Married in the said chapel according to the rites and ceremonies of the Independent Dissenters by me, Charles Baker. This marriage was solemnized between us Alfred Simper, Elizabeth Clare in the presence of us, Anna Clare, Lydia Clare, George Simper.*

Alfred was a violinist who played with various local ensembles, including Salisbury Musical Society. Unusually for the time, the Simpers seemed to have had a small family – Caleb only had one known sibling, Alfred Clare Simper, five years his junior.

As far as we know Simper had no formal musical training, though his first job that was recorded (certainly not his first employment) was as manager of E. J. Sparks & Co, a music warehouse based at 12 High Street, Worcester (just two doors away from Elgar Brothers, the music shop owned by Edward Elgar's father and uncle). It has been assumed that he moved to Worcester shortly after his marriage in 1879 to Emily Yates, a 30-year-old Australian who was living at the time with her aunt and uncle in Wilton, just a few miles from Barford.

By now you are getting very short of time. The temptation may be just to hand in the pasted text. But even a few minutes spent on changing it can make a huge amount of difference, not only making the text your own by changing words and phrasing you would never use (so making it more acceptable to your teacher) but also making it better than it was to start with. You would never sit down and write the text above, so take a few minutes turn it into your own work. A couple of quick passes through it can make all the difference.

If possible, print the text out on paper. Read through the whole thing to get a general feeling for it. Highlight anything that sounds or looks strange to you. Look for spellings that might be from a different type of English, look for terms or locations you aren't familiar with, and for words and phrases that you would never use in a million years.

Here's the same text with some highlights assuming the person with the assignment is from the US:

Caleb Simper was born on **12 September 1856** in the **village** of Barford St. Martin, a **village** on the Shaftsbury road to the West of Salisbury in **Wiltshire**. His parents were Alfred Simper, a "boot and shoemaker," and Elizabeth Clare.

Thanks to John Chryssides for this information from Simper's parents' wedding certificate:

> *1852 Marriage solemnized at Crow Lane Chapel, Wilton in the District of Wilton Union **in the county of Wilts**. Second of September 1852 Alfred Simper 31 years Bachelor, Shoemaker, Barford St Martin (father John Simper, **Labourer**) and Elizabeth Clare 32 years Spinster, Barford St Martin (father George Clare, Dairyman). Married in the said chapel according to the rites and ceremonies of the Independent Dissenters by me, Charles Baker. This marriage was solemnized between us Alfred Simper, Elizabeth Clare in the presence of us, Anna Clare, Lydia Clare, George Simper.*

Alfred was a violinist who played with **various local ensembles**, including Salisbury Musical Society. Unusually for the time, the Simpers seemed to have had a small family – Caleb only had one known sibling, Alfred Clare Simper, five years his junior.

As far as we know Simper had no formal musical training, though his first job that was recorded (**certainly not his first employment**) was as manager of E. J. Sparks & Co, a music warehouse based at 12 High Street, Worcester (just two doors away from Elgar Brothers, the music shop owned by Edward

> Elgar's father and uncle). It has been assumed that he moved
> to Worcester shortly after his marriage in 1879 to Emily Yates,
> a 30-year-old Australian who was living at the time with her
> aunt and uncle in Wilton, just a few miles from Barford.

I've not highlighted everything that could be changed, but I have picked out a few examples. The date "12 September 1856" can be re-written September 12, 1856 to put it into the regular US date format. I've noticed that in that first sentence, the word "village" is repeated quite close to the first occurrence. This reads clumsily, so it would be best to knock out "the village of" so it reads "was born on September 12, 1856 in Barford St. Martin, a village . . .". The writer of the original document thought it was enough to say that Barford St. Martin was in Wiltshire, but we don't know where the composer comes from, so it might be better to say Wiltshire, England. Even better, we could start the whole thing by saying "English composer Caleb Simper . . .".

Next there comes an acknowledgement of help from someone called John Chryssides – there is no reason why this should appear in your assignment, and it makes it look very obviously like cut and pasted material. Next we see "in the county of Wilts." Is this "Wilts" a typing error for Wiltshire? A quick web search on "county of Wilts" reveals that Wilts is a common abbreviation of Wiltshire, so this shouldn't be changed, as it's in a quotation. Don't fix apparent mistakes in a quotation, unless it's obvious that the quotation has been mistyped. Similarly, while you'd want to change "labourer" to "laborer" in normal text, because it's in a quote you should leave the British spelling.

Finally I've picked out two phrases as examples of ones that might not seem right to you, though there will be plenty more that aren't how you would write and you would need to change. The author says that Alfred played with "various local ensembles" – perhaps you might prefer "a lot of local groups" or "several nearby bands". Then there's the aside "certainly not his first employment". This comes across as stiff and formal. You might prefer to take it out entirely, or to replace it with "he had other ones before" or something similar.

So after that first quick pass, a piece of work that might only have taken a minute, the text becomes:

English composer Caleb Simper was born on September 12, 1856 in Barford St. Martin, a village on the Shaftsbury road to the West of Salisbury in Wiltshire. His parents were Alfred Simper, a "boot and shoemaker," and Elizabeth Clare.

> Simper's parents' wedding certificate gives this information: *1852 Marriage solemnized at Crow Lane Chapel, Wilton in the District of Wilton Union in the county of Wilts. Second of September 1852 Alfred Simper 31 years Bachelor, Shoemaker, Barford St Martin (father John Simper, Labourer) and Elizabeth Clare 32 years Spinster, Barford St Martin (father George Clare, Dairyman). Married in the said chapel according to the rites and ceremonies of the Independent Dissenters by me, Charles Baker. This marriage was solemnized between us Alfred Simper, Elizabeth Clare in the presence of us, Anna Clare, Lydia Clare, George Simper.*

Alfred was a violinist who played with several nearby groups, including Salisbury Musical Society. Unusually for the time, the Simpers seemed to have had a small family – Caleb only had one known sibling, Alfred Clare Simper, five years his junior.

As far as we know Simper had no formal musical training, though his first job that was recorded was as manager of E. J. Sparks & Co, a music warehouse based at 12 High Street, Worcester (just two doors away from Elgar Brothers, the music shop owned by Edward Elgar's father and uncle). It has been assumed that he moved to Worcester shortly after his marriage in 1879 to Emily Yates, a 30-year-old Australian who was living at the time with her aunt and uncle in Wilton, just a few miles from Barford.

That's the emergency fixes in place, but it's still not really your own words. Take a second pass through, sentence by sentence. Read each sentence through and replace it with your own wording. Sometimes you might need to change the order of things around a little to get a better flow. Here's how it might look after that second pass:

English composer Caleb Simper was born on September 12, 1856 in Barford St. Martin, a village near Salisbury in Wiltshire. His father was Alfred Simper, who made boots and shoes, and his mother was Elizabeth Clare.

This is what we can find from Alfred and Elizabeth's marriage certificate:

> 1852 Marriage solemnized at Crow Lane Chapel, Wilton in the District of Wilton Union in the county of Wilts. Second of September 1852 Alfred Simper 31 years Bachelor, Shoemaker, Barford St Martin (father John Simper, Labourer) and Elizabeth Clare 32 years Spinster, Barford St Martin (father George Clare, Dairyman). Married in the said chapel according to the rites and ceremonies of the Independent Dissenters by me, Charles Baker. This marriage was solemnized between us Alfred Simper, Elizabeth Clare in the presence of us, Anna Clare, Lydia Clare, George Simper.

Caleb's father played violin with orchestras and bands in the area, including the Salisbury Musical Society. As far as we know, Caleb only had one brother or sister, Alfred Clare Simper, born five years after him – a very small family for the time.

Caleb's first job that can be traced was as manager of a music warehouse in Worcester called E. J. Sparks. This was practically next door to Elgar Brothers, the music shop owned by the father and uncle of the more famous composer Edward Elgar. With a job like that, Caleb had probably had some musical training, but no details have been found. We don't know exactly when Caleb moved from Barford St. Martin to Worcester, but it seems likely it was soon after he got married to Emily Yates, an Australian who he met at her aunt's house in Wilton, a few miles from Barford. The wedding was in 1879, when Caleb was 23, seven years younger than Emily.

Some of the changes are quite subtle – the first sentence, for example. In others I have been more direct, for example in the introduction to the text from the wedding certificate. Note how at the end I have reused information in a different way. Instead of saying Emily was 30, I have said that Caleb was 23, and he was seven years younger than Emily. I have also dropped the uncle from Emily's "aunt and uncle" – no real need to mention both, it just sounds clumsy. I have also cheated a little. The original didn't say that Caleb met Emily at her aunt's house, but it seems quite likely, and it read well. This is acceptable if it's just a descriptive piece, but if you were expected to write an accurate historical account, that was an assumption, and you would have to mention it, by saying something like "it seems likely that he met her at her aunt's house."

Under real time pressure this is probably all I could achieve. If I had more time, then it would have been much better to go for a *collate and write* approach, but at least I managed to get something that was much more my own than the original website with only a few minutes' work.

Never use this approach for course work or other material which is going to count towards an examination or degree. Even though it's not as bad as cut and paste, it is still recognizable as being very closely related to the original. In the example above, the teacher or lecturer would be aware of this website, because there genuinely are very few websites about Caleb Simper, and he or she would check your work against the original as a matter of course. It's not worth risking being accused of cheating.

Collect and modify

Good for – a quick overview where no depth is required and there is time pressure to get something finished quickly.

Pros – quick, easy, and produces a result with some personalization.

Cons – a lack of input, based on too few sources, is unlikely to be structured to meet your requirements and there are still elements of plagiarism (copying).

Collate and write

If the topic is a new one to you, this is likely to be the most effective approach – and it's essential that you use this, or the *write and refine* approach when doing anything that will count towards an examination or degree; it's the only way of making sure that this is truly your own work, and you won't be accused of copying.

Collate and write is the approach we have already met in the previous chapter. Given your brief, collect together as much information as you can from different websites and (if necessary) books. Work out an outline for your assignment, and structure your information within it. Condense the information down, removing duplication and leaving only the bare bones. Then write your own piece, filling in the outline section by section, based on the information but not copying it.

! Hot tip – leave it

I have written more than twenty books and numerous articles for magazines and newspapers. If you were to ask me for the single most important tip I have for making sure what you've written is as good as you can make it, then it comes down to two simple words: leave it.

I don't mean give up. I mean once you've written it, put it to one side. Leave it for a while. Then come back to it with a fresh eye, read it through and improve it.

If you are writing something short like an essay, this can be a matter of leaving it to the next day. If it's something longer, like a project, leave it for around a week. Then when you come back to it you are much more likely to spot mistakes and to think of improvements than you would be when you've just written it.

Of course you don't always have enough time to leave it, but if you do (and you can make this possible by doing the work soon after it has been set, then coming back to it near when it's due in), I can guarantee you will get a better result.

It sounds like a lot of hard work, but it doesn't have to take a long time, and the *collect and write* approach is much more likely to achieve a good result that you can really be proud of.

Collate and write

Good for – practically anything! Reports, articles, assignments, homework, all the way up to full-length books.

Pros – based on a wide range of information from multiple sources, and the result is your own work.

Cons – can be slow to assemble, and the structure may not be ideal as it is a compromise between your brief and the information that you collect.

Write and refine

If the topic is one you already know really well – perhaps a subject that you have been studying for some time – it may be that you can write much of the text without looking things up on the web, in textbooks or anywhere else. There is still a need to plan out what you intend to say and how the report (or whatever it is) is going to be structured – but you may not need to do the research up front.

The great thing about *write and refine* is that you can put together a piece of work that flows much more effectively than anything that is assembled piece by piece from research. Often the best pieces of writing shorter than around 3,000 words are written in one go, rather than piecemeal. It's hard to write anything longer than that at a single sitting (this book, for example, couldn't have been written this way), and for many people even 3,000 words is impossibly long to produce all at once, but having structured the piece it's possible you can identify a suitable section of it that you can write uninterrupted.

If, as you go, there is something that you don't know, whether it's a simple fact (what date did this event happen? for instance) or a need for a particular chunk of text that you can't fill in, don't stop to do it – you will break the flow. Instead, make a note that you need to return and fill in some information later. Either put a flag in the text in a particular format (for example a special word like !!UPDATE!! that you can search for), or use a note facility, like Word's Insert Comment, to put in a clear visual flag that you need some information slotted in place. It is essential if you have any doubt about what you are putting in that you flag it up for a check.

Once you have that basic piece of work, you can then go into the refinement phase. Fill in the specifics that you have flagged up, but then do a general sweep of research, pulling in useful information. Work through each of the sources. If you come across something that is missing from your piece you can add in anything from a few words to a whole section. Watch out, also, for anything that disagrees with what you have said. You might be right, rather than the website, but you need to check your facts.

Here's the start of an attempt at our "mystery" brief: *Leland Stanford, founder of Stanford University, once bet on a flying horse. Or did he? Explain.* This happens to be something that came up in a book I wrote about the pioneer motion picture photographer, Eadweard Muybridge, so I can make a reasonable attempt without initially researching – but as it was a while since I looked at the material, I need to fill in some gaps.

Betting on a flying horse

"Can a horse fly?" might sound like something out of a song in the Disney film *Dumbo* [CHECK], but in fact it was a serious consideration in the second half of the nineteenth century. No one was quite sure whether a galloping horse ever had all four feet off the ground at the same time. Such was the interest that it's said Leland Stanford, founder of Stanford University [FULL NAME?] bet [AMOUNT & WORTH NOW] in [DATE]. The other parties in the bet were said to be [NAMES], but in fact the whole thing seems to have been made up. It really happened like this . . .

I normally use Word's Insert Comment feature, because you can then use the Reviewing toolbar to jump from comment to comment as you fill in the information and because it puts the comments in the margin without disturbing the flow (and it looks pretty). But if you don't want to use this, or your word processor doesn't have that feature, just use a punctuation that makes your notes stand out like the !!UPDATE!! I suggested earlier, or square brackets in my example above. It's then easy to use a search facility in the word processor, or just to scan over the text by eye and look for information that needs filling in with a little research.

In my example, I thought it was *Dumbo* that contained the song about never seeing an elephant fly, but I wanted to check. I knew that Stanford University wasn't the university's full name, but couldn't remember exactly what it was. The bet was something like $25,000, but I wasn't sure what the exact figure was, or what $25,000 then was worth now. And I had a total blank when it came to the names of the other people involved in the bet. But by just letting the piece flow, and not worrying about the information I didn't have to hand, I could write it quickly and effectively, then fill in the details later.

I ought to stress that *write and refine* isn't just about filling in the gaps of what you can remember. You do still need to do a proper web search and collect and sift through the information to see what's missing from your piece. When you do the research, you will find information you just never knew about that will have to be slotted in. You will have to change some of what you have written and may even have to throw some of it away. But if you already know the subject quite well, you probably won't have to bin too much of it – and what you have will probably work much better for writing it in a continuous fashion.

Write and refine

Good for – reports, articles, assignments, and homework where the topic is well known to you already.

Pros – the result is your own work and builds around your preferred structure. Has a natural flow.

Cons – the piece may need considerable re-writing if you weren't as right as you thought. Mistakes may slip through.

Editing down

Whichever approach you take you may find that you end up with a piece that is too long. If you have been given a specific number of words or pages, now is the time to check. If you have overwritten (written too many words), don't worry – that's a good thing. It's what most professional journalists do. When I'm writing for a magazine I will normally write between 20 and 100 percent more than was requested. That doesn't mean I'm going to submit an article that is too long – for many editors, overlong pieces are worse than pieces that are too short, because it's easier to fill in with a picture or a sidebar than it is to cut text down on a subject you don't know as well as the author. But it gives me the material to make a better piece by some judicious editing.

Almost every bit of writing initially contains text that it would be better to do without. If you have overwritten your piece, you have the opportunity to trim it down, to make it sleeker and more graceful, without losing any of the good stuff. A few quick passes through the text, cutting vigorously but with care, can make all the difference between a so-so piece of writing and an exciting article that encourages the reader to keep going.

First, go for the redundant words. **Little, sniveling words that do not really deliver anything more for the text that you have written**. Destroy them mercilessly. Take that previous sentence beginning "Little, sniveling".. Let's give it a trim. Although it probably wasn't necessary to use both "little" and "sniveling" at the start, the two adjectives give the sentence a kick start and I would like to keep them in. But "do not" is a little clumsy, and unless I was writing very formally, I think I would prefer "don't" in this context. That word "really" does nothing at all for the sentence. It's redundant.

Then what about that "you have written" bit at the end? Isn't it obvious we're talking about the text you had written? I can gather that from the context. In fact it might be better still to drop "for the text" as well. Once I've done that, it might be better to change "more" to "new". So I end up with this. **Little, sniveling words that don't deliver anything new**. I have lost 9 words from 17 and produced a sentence that is more pithy, more to the point and more readable.

If you were only a little over your target, a pass through doing this sort of trimming may well be enough – but you can't depend on it. If you still have more than a few dozen words to get rid of, you will probably have to take out a whole sentence or paragraph. Look for a paragraph that can either be replaced by a single sentence or be disposed of altogether. This is probably the hardest thing to do. You put it in there for a reason, so you want to keep it. But make sure that the reason was to make the piece as a whole better. Often you will find that a paragraph you can remove without much impact on the piece was just slipped in to show how clever you are, or to highlight some pet topic that hasn't much to do with your theme. You are better off without it.

I don't write particularly flowery prose, but I have never yet found an article I've written that can't have up to half its length trimmed to good effect. It might be you do everything I've said and still end up a few hundred words too long. Go back and do it again. It might take several passes, but eventually you will get it down to the right length. And as long as you haven't taken so much out that your piece lacks meaning or readability, you are very likely to have improved it in the process.

Padding up

A harder problem you will sometimes have to face is when you have written everything you need to write on a subject – and your piece is still much too short. If you are lucky it may be simply that you haven't got enough material. Then the solution is simple enough – to go back and collect some more. But this isn't always the case. As with reducing the length of your text, there are a number of steps to take.

First, take the lesson of the magazine editor. Can you bring the piece up to length by adding in a couple of illustrations? These have to be relevant, but if you need to fill up page space, rather than increase the number of words, a few good pictures will make all the difference. Use the magazine trick, also, of employing boxes.

> **! Hot tip – what's in the box?**
>
> A box or sidebar is a mini article that is outside the flow of the main piece of text. It can be used to illustrate a point in more detail, or to define unfamiliar terms, or to provide interaction, like an exercise. All these are possibilities for adding boxes to pad out your text (and, of course, unlike illustrations any words in the box count towards your overall total). If you can't come up with any supplementary material to go in a box, you can always use one to present a quick summary of your piece. Tell them what it's about and what your conclusions are.
>
> Other popular things to put in a box:

- lists (like this one)
- a short set of key points
- asides
- biographies of major characters.

Look out for the opportunity to add new sections and some structuring (like a contents page and sub-headings if it's a long piece). See if you can throw in a little more description. But when doing padding, don't reverse the principle from the previous section by adding in redundant words. You can probably get away with removing a few contractions (turning "can't" into "can not," for instance – but make sure it still reads smoothly), but padding in the sense of shoving in lots of unnecessary adjectives and non-words will reduce the value of your piece. Don't dilute it with rubbish.

Turning information into original work

For some, the idea of taking a set of facts and turning it into a piece of original work – and really that's what most creative projects, assignments, and homework are about – comes very naturally. For others it's a huge challenge even to understand that there's something here worth doing. When I describe what I do as a non-fiction writer, researching a subject, then writing a book, such people say, "But isn't that just copying what other people have already said?" I have to show that I'm doing much more than copying.

This is a challenge that faces non-fiction writers every day. Novelists have it easy (in this sense). They just sit down and write from their imagination. But writing non-fiction needs a basis in fact. Practically any subject you might want to write an article or a book about has already got *something* written about it. And those books will form part of your research, as will tracking down primary sources (the original stuff other people have written about).

But you, as writer, have the opportunity – more than that, you have the responsibility – to take that basic information and add to it, putting your own slant on it. You have to make it *yours*. There are four basic ways that you can make a piece of "off the shelf" information into something of your own:

1   Make the information more readable.
2   Present the information in a different way.
3   Pull together elements of the information that don't otherwise
    appear together.
4   Put your own opinions alongside the factual content.

. . . hopefully you will use all of these. Let's look at each in a little
more detail.

Making the information more readable

This is the primary job of the popular science writer, the news
journalist and many others who have to take a complex or messily
covered subject and make it more approachable. It may be that the
information you are presenting comes from a technical source that
assumes the reader already knows a lot about the subject, and is written
with all the passion and flair of a contents label. It may be that the
information comes from some government report, packed with jargon
and unnecessary detail, and cursed with so much dullness that you
need to prop your eyelids open to read it. Or it could be that the only
descriptions of the topic are in textbooks, rarely known for their
excellent presentation.

Your job here is similar to that of many successful businesses –
adding value. You are going to take some raw material and do some
hard labor on it, so the person who then reads *your* version doesn't
have to do that grunt work. It's like the difference between eating roast
chicken in a restaurant and buying an unprepared bird, complete with
feathers, head and innards. You are going to do the preparation, cook
it up and serve it with vegetables on the side. (Metaphorically speaking.
I'm not expecting you to get to work in the kitchen here.) Take a look
at this unprepared chicken:

> ### From *Superluminal Signaling by Photonic Tunneling* (Günter Nimtz)
>
> Photonic tunneling has found much theoretical and applied
> interest recently. Superluminal photonic pulse transmission
> and reflection have been presented of microwave and infrared

frequencies. Presumably superluminal photonic and electronic devices can become reality soon. The author introduces new experimental and theoretical data on superluminal tunneling. Data of reflection by tunneling barriers have evidenced the nonlocal properties of tunneling. An empirical relation was found for the photonic tunneling time independent of the system in question. The relation seems to be universal for all tunneling processes. The outstanding property of superluminal velocity can be applied to speed up photonic modulation and transmission as well as to improve micro electronic devices.

Don't worry if you gave up reading the box above. It's not surprising if you did – it's hard going. Yet this is pretty friendly stuff as academic papers go. It's the abstract, the "readable" summary at the start of the paper, rather than the detail, and it's written by someone who tends to write papers in something close to plain English. Let's see how I can do a little preparation on those words to get them ready for consumption.

I need to replace some of the jargon with words that are less painful to the reader. This isn't necessarily a matter of simply replacing a word with another. The jargon may be there because there aren't any other words to describe what's happening. In that case I will have to put in a line or two of explanatory text. For example, the whole thing starts with the words "Photonic tunneling," merrily assuming we know what this is all about, where actually most of us would already have given up halfway through that first word. So I would have to say something like: "Tiny particles, like photons of light, have the strange ability to pass through a barrier, disappearing one side, and appearing the other without ever traveling through the space in between. When light does this, it's called photonic tunneling."

When it comes to the rest of that first sentence, "Photonic tunneling has found much theoretical and applied interest recently," it's not so much that it is too technical, just that it is very stiff and formal, the traditional language of the academic paper, but not of good, real world writing. Instead of saying "It has found much theoretical and applied interest recently," we could say, "Many scientists are now working on the theory behind it, and are trying to find a practical use for it." Okay, it's not prize-winning literature, but it is better because it's written more naturally, with the active participant, the scientist, in the sentence, rather than modestly hidden away as they tend to be in papers.

Just by explaining or rewording jargon and turning the text into a more easy to read form, we can convert the information into this:

Based on *Superluminal Signaling by Photonic Tunneling* (Günter Nimtz)

Tiny particles, like photons of light, have the strange ability to pass through a barrier, disappearing one side, and appearing the other without ever traveling through the space in between. When light does this, it's called photonic tunneling. Many scientists are now working on the theory behind this tunneling, and are trying to find a practical use for it. The hope is that there will soon be commercial applications.

In his paper, Professor Nimtz gives some new results from experiments, and develops a theory to explain these results. All the evidence is that the light that tunnels through the barriers manages somehow to do this without passing through the space inside the barrier. Nimtz found that the time taken to go through the barrier wasn't affected by the type or size of barrier used – it's always the same. Because it effectively travels faster than light, there's a chance to use this effect to make faster and better electronic devices.

My version has almost all the information from the first (I dropped the little part about microwave and infrared frequencies as not being of relevance to my audience, again something you can do). But it is a totally different piece of text, and one that is more readable by a member of the general public.

Of course I was only able to do that because I already knew something about physics and about photonic tunneling, having interviewed Professor Nimtz and read a lot about the subject. If you were starting from scratch you would have to read up some background material and find more information on some of those key terms like "photonic" and "superluminal" – but the most important thing I was doing was making the writing style more approachable.

This isn't the book to teach you everything you need to know about effective writing, but there are a few key points it's worth remembering if you are trying to make some technical (or boring) information more readable:

- **Use common words** Reduce the level of jargon. If you have to use a jargon term because it would be very clumsy to describe what it means every time, explain it.
- **Avoid other technical special language and terms** Keep it in plain English. If I'm explaining a piece of math that involves a formula, for instance, I would avoid using "x" and "y" and all that stuff wherever possible. Use words instead. Of course, if your assignment is not about explaining mathematics, just about doing the sums, stick to the formulas – that's the whole point of them.
- **Give good, specific and interesting examples** Show how something is used, or what it's about, by giving specific examples. You will see this happening on TV news all the time. Instead of just telling you about a tax change (boring!) they will demonstrate it using a pile of coins as if it was a monthly salary, then will interview a real family and show what effect the tax change will have on their lifestyle.
- **Give some context** This is the crucial difference between, for example, popular science books and science text books. The textbook will just tell you that $E = mc^2$, but the popular science book will tell you what Einstein meant, how he reached this conclusion and quite possibly what he had breakfast that morning. As human beings we are social animals and like to know about other people. (This explains the popularity of soap operas and reality TV shows.) People turn facts into stories, so bring people into your facts.
- **Keep sentences short** I don't mean everything has to be delivered in little staccato outbursts. Like this. Not at all. But do break things down into short sentences, and fairly short paragraphs, because if you are tempted to run on and on as this sentence seems to be doing, your reader could get lost or bored, or eventually, after attempting to cope with one too many clauses (even worse if you have parentheses (that's brackets) as well), may give up entirely and lose the will to live.
- **Color your information** Yes, you are trying to get across facts or opinions, but make sure there are some adjectives in there when you are describing objects, or adverbs when describing action.

Make it live. By turning a dull, factual statement into something more interesting you can do a lot to make it your own.

- **Forget the "scientific detached" style (unless ordered otherwise)** Unless you are specifically told to do so, don't use the traditional "scientific detached" style. This is a very artificial way of writing, used to give a sense of objectivity to a paper. So instead, for instance, of saying "we heated the liquid to boiling point and saw a purple vapor emerge from the tube," scientists are trained to say, "the water was heated to boiling point and a purple vapor was seen to emerge from the tube." The first version is more readable and less artificial. There is no benefit in using the contorted structures of the second version to make it impersonal. But you will have to use this style where told to do so.

- **Have fun** Perhaps the most important tip in making your prose readable is to have fun writing it. With any luck, your audience will also enjoy themselves. This doesn't mean be silly and try to force jokes in everywhere. Just enjoy doing the writing.

I've said it before, but it really needs repeating, because this is about the biggest single thing you can do to make sure that what you've written is readable. Take a break from it, then come back and read it through yourself. Don't just pour the words onto the page and then hand your assignment in. Leave a little time after you've written it (ideally at least 24 hours, though I realize this isn't always possible), then read it through yourself. Again, if possible, do the read through on paper rather than on the screen. Imagine you were someone who has never seen it before. Look out for dull and incomprehensible bits and re-write them. (You can also spot spelling mistakes and the like along the way, but the main thing here is readability.) It needn't take long, but it can make all the difference to the finished result.

Presenting the information in a different way

The mere action of making your text more readable is, of course, one aspect of presenting the information in a different way, but that is only a starting point. Here are a few more essential techniques to take an uninspiring collection of facts and make them more approachable:

- **Use a picture** As we saw in chapter 4, you can't beat a picture to get across a lot of information in a small amount of space.

Illustrate with photographs, diagrams, anything that will make the information more visible. Choose the illustrations appropriately, though. This isn't a matter of using pictures for the sake of it, but to put something across that might not otherwise be appreciated.

- **Chart it** One specific way of turning information into a more visual communication is to produce charts of sets of numbers. These can be very effective, particularly to put across trends and to get an overview of a large collection of numbers. Not everyone relates well to charts, so it's a good idea to leave the numbers in an appendix at the back of your report. However, most readers will find charts help them to understand information.
- **Structure it differently** Almost any set of information can be approached a different way. Is a timeline appropriate? Can you tie the information to different people who have been involved, or does it fit better to how the subject area is normally divided up? For instance, if I was doing the essay on teleportation, I could structure it by the scientists involved, or the scientific principles. I could break it down by fiction and non-fiction, or keep the fiction and non-fiction together, looking at different ways teleportation could be used. Look at different ways to structure what you've got. Bear in mind, though, that there may be a best way to approach things. Biographies, for example, usually work best in time order, and though writers might try to be different by structuring in a different way, the result is usually confusing and unhelpful.
- **Use bullet points** Bullet points can help break information up and give it more structure. Alternatively, use tables or whatever different style suits the information.

Charting troubled waters

Let's compare four different charts presenting the same information. What we're looking at is a set of sales figures for something or other (it doesn't matter what – sales of inflatable dragons, maybe) for the years 1955 to 1970. We want to see how things have changed over the years. What has happened to sales levels?

This first attempt, a pie chart (opposite), is a total disaster. It looks more like King Arthur's table than a useful presentation of information. A pie chart is a great way to compare a few pieces of data to see how they compare in size, but it's useless when they are all similar

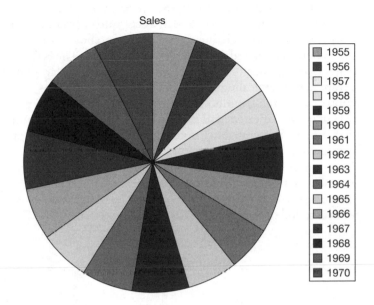

in scale, and it gives no idea of a progression through time. It's impossible to see from this chart if there's any trend in the sales, and if so, what it is.

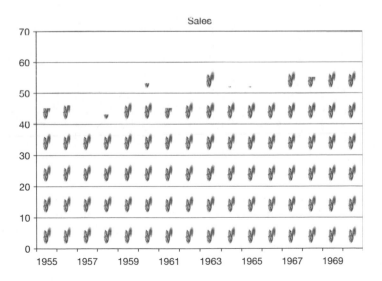

The good news is that presenting the information on a chart with two axes (that's the plural of axis, not of ax) is much better than a pie chart for something that changes with time (see above). I can scan along from left to right and see how things have gone. The bad news, though, is that I decided to be clever and use arty little dollar symbols to indicate that we're dealing with money.

Unfortunately, these symbols make it very difficult to be certain just what is being indicated, and that mass of squashed $ signs simply confuses the eye. You probably can't even tell that they were meant to be dollar signs, and they add nothing to the presentation.

This approach of using stacks of "something meaningful" in a chart is a mistake that's often made by the wizards who dream up TV graphics. The presentation is made too pretty, because it can be – and the result is to hide what the chart is supposed to tell us.

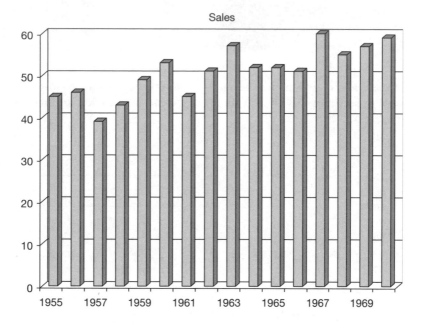

The chart above is exactly the same as the previous one, but has solid bars instead of bitty $ signs. Now we're getting somewhere. It's fine to use a little graphic artiness and make the bars three dimensional, but the values are much clearer now that we have proper bars. This approach makes it easy to pick out something like the worst years (1957 and 1958) or the best (1967 and 1970). But don't forget an even simpler alternative, just because it is so simple – the line chart below.

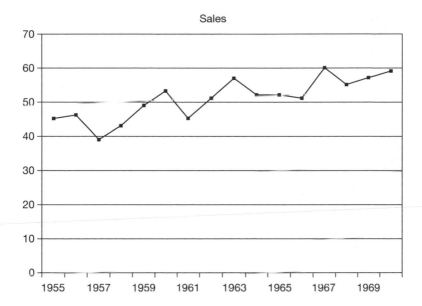

Sales

If you want to follow how something is changing over time, you can't beat a line chart to help your eye follow the trend. It might be boringly simple, it might be something you could have done with a crayon when you were 10. But it doesn't matter, the line chart does the job. Here, I can see that the sales are heading gradually upwards. If it isn't obvious, you can ask your charting program to produce a trend line which will emphasize how the data is changing.

In the end, the choice is up to you, but make sure your graphic or chart clearly illustrates the facts. Don't be tempted, as TV news often is, to distort a change to make it more visually obvious. This is most clearly done by only taking part of the data. So we might use a chart like the one at the top of the next page. This chart is designed to indicate the worrying way that crime is increasing. Look at how it's shooting up! Unfortunately, two points aren't enough to tell you *anything* meaningful. The other chart on page 130 looks at the bigger picture. Now we can see just how deceptive the first chart was. In fact, the rate is clearly falling, not rising. You won't often catch TV

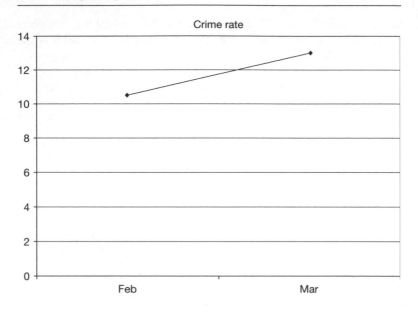

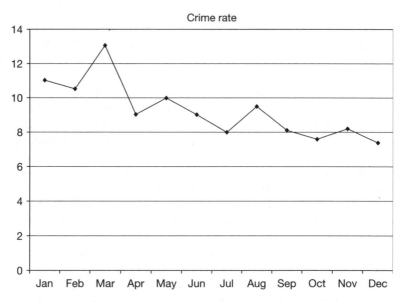

shows being quite so unsubtle about their graphics, but the chart opposite illustrates a trick they use all the time. Look at the truly dramatic rise in crime rate that appears to have happened in the following year. Okay, there are variations along the way, including that

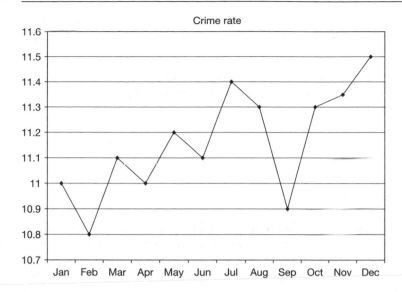

big dip in September (presumably all the criminals were on vacation), but the trend is drastically up, isn't it? No, it isn't. The chart below contains the same information on a more honest scale. Although the crime rate is very slightly rising, seen in proportion to the total value, the growth is small.

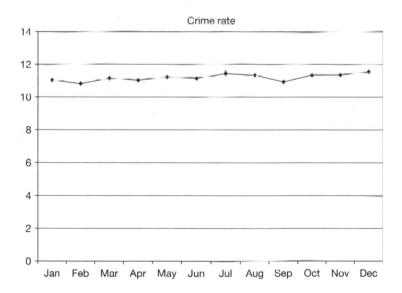

The choice is up to you – but it's best to be honest. Present your information in a striking way, but not with the intention to mislead.

Pulling together elements of the information that don't otherwise appear together

Stand by for an amazing thought. In principle, someone could own a library that contained every book that was ever written, and every book that ever will be written, *before those books were even dreamed of, or their authors had been born*! Want to read the next book by your favorite author? It's already in that library. What's more, that same library would contain every bit of scientific knowledge that will ever be discovered. Imagine 10,000 years in the future, maybe there will be a limitless source of energy, a way to fly across the galaxy, a solution to all the big scientific problems we have today. Our library will have details of that too. Right now. And most amazingly of all, you don't need to be intelligent to assemble this library. Anyone who can write a simple computer program can produce a piece of software that will generate the library with no human assistance.

There is a catch – but you would expect that, wouldn't you?

Here's how it's done. Most books are no more than 100,000 words long – we won't bother with the really long ones. Including spaces, on average that'll be about 600,000 characters (letters, numbers, etc.) in each book. So all we do is write a computer program that generates the books. First it produces a book that's all spaces. Then a book with an A as the first character, and the other 599,999 characters are spaces. Then a book with a space, then an A, then the rest of the book is totally filled with spaces. And so on. And on.

When the program has worked through every possible combination of As and spaces, all the way up to a book full of As, then it can throw Bs into the mix. And so it goes. It will take a very long time. Longer than the lifetime of the universe to date. But eventually, in principle, this idiot program will have generated every single book up to 600,000 characters long that has been or ever will be written.

Imagine that you had let this program run for the ridiculously long time it would have to work to churn out every book. You now have a library with every single book that ever has been or ever will be in it, including the book you are now reading. (You could have saved yourself some cash there.) Unfortunately, there will also be many, many more books in the library that are gibberish. Total rubbish. So you *could* reach out and pick up a superb piece of wisdom, or the best novel ever – but the problem is knowing which book to pick.

On a smaller scale, the world of information on the internet (and libraries and all the rest) is a bit like that (though hopefully rather less of the books and web pages contain absolute gibberish). It's quite possible that everything someone needs to know on a subject is out there, but there's a fact in one place, some detail in other, a description somewhere else, and a picture in yet another location. One of the essential ways to make information your own is to take bits from different places and pull them together in a way that is unique. Not just a unique order or combination, but in a way that one piece of information is complemented and made better by another.

It's not so surprising that it's possible. All Western music is made with variants of just 12 notes. All writing is made up of 27 basic characters (and a few subtleties). You can make something worthwhile and important by bringing together information in new ways. You might find a very basic bit of information – a chemical formula, a historical event, or whatever, in one place. In another you might find some information about the way that formula was discovered, or the people who took part in the event. Put them together and you get synergy – the effect where a combination of things is more valuable or effective than the parts taken individually. (You've got synergy yourself – as a person, there is more to you than just a collection of inanimate molecules.)

The formula might be both easier to understand and mean more if you know how it was discovered. You might be able to say something about why the event happened, or what its implications were, if you knew more about the people involved. Neither of the bits of information you've used were so valuable in their original context – it's your insight in bringing them together that makes something new and interesting. So one of the simplest ways to produce something new and original is to pull together information from a range of different sources, as the techniques and tools in the previous chapter will help you do. Look for pieces of information that haven't been put together before and support each other in a new way. Like the composer, assembling new combinations and sequences of those same old notes, you can come up with something fresh and interesting.

Doing it for real – it's all Greek to me

Here's a simple example of what I'm talking about. When I wrote my book *A Brief History of Infinity*, I read lots of books on infinity and the development of mathematical ideas. Most of the books said that the Ancient Greeks had two different ways to represent numbers, but very little was said about how the Greeks handled fractions, which would be essential when looking at infinite series of numbers.

I found a website that had some helpful information, but not what I was looking for, and emailed the website owner. He came back with a small detail, but not what I really wanted. I then discovered the email address of a lecturer on the history of math from another website. I emailed him with my question. He admitted he wasn't too hot on Greek mathematics, but he knew a man who was, and gave me a contact. Finally I reached another academic who knew all there was to know. It would be nice to say that he gave me the answer on a plate, but instead he said, "You'll find it all in my book," giving details of what to look for. So with a little library work, I finally had the best answer.

Now there had been a good few books written on infinity before mine. All of them had mentioned the Greeks' work on infinite series of fractions – but not one of them had anything to say about how the Greeks *understood* fractions. And it was quite different to the way we use them. Instead of saying "a third," for instance, they would say "the third part." This sounds like just playing with words, but where we think of something divided into three thirds, the Greeks were visualizing a whole shape, which you would need three of to make the result – and this subtly different way of looking at it colored their attitude to number and math.

By combining the information from the academics' book with the more widely available information available on infinity, I was able to cast new light on how the Greeks used these infinite series.

It was only a small point, but in the example above, by pulling together this obscure historical work with more mainstream information on the Greeks' infinite series, I had made something new, given a new insight. And it's something everyone can do.

A good way to spot the opportunities to combine a new piece of information with an existing piece, is to read what you've already got and ask yourself, "What questions does this leave me with?" Then look for different sources to answer those questions. Here's a simple piece of history of science fact as an example of how to do this. It's a quote from my book on infinity.

Brownian motion

Brownian motion is the theory that describes the way small particles like dust are buffeted around in a random way by collision with molecules.

The name dates back to the 1820s, when the English botanist James Brown noticed that pollen grains in a drop of water, viewed under a microscope, jumped and danced around in an unpredictable fashion. This was originally assumed to be some characteristic of the life in the pollen, but it was soon found that ancient pollen with no possibility of life remaining behaved exactly the same way. It was in 1877 that Desaulx proposed the correct reason – that it was the natural thermal motion of the molecules in the liquid that was causing them to collide with the much bigger pollen grains and making them move, and not until 1905 that Einstein provided a mathematical description of what was happening.

Imagine you'd got this quote from my book as one of your initial pieces of information. Here are some questions you might ask, and in providing answers from different sources and combining it with the information you had already got from *A Brief History of Infinity*, could produce something new:

- Exactly when did Brown do his work?
- Who was James Brown? What was his life like? What other discoveries did he make?

- What sort of pollen did Brown use?
- Where did they get ancient pollen from (and who studied ancient pollen)?
- Who was Desaulx? Where did he come from? What else did he do?
- What is natural thermal motion?
- How do the collisions make the pollen grains move?
- What was Einstein doing in 1905? Why did he choose to study Brownian motion?
- What sort of mathematical description did he come up with?

. . . and so on. Answer a few of these questions from different sources and you will start to get a new mix of information.

Sometimes, by following up these questions you might find something that makes the whole topic more fascinating. The ancient pollen was taken from Egyptian tombs – so there would be a great opportunity for description there. But it won't always be easy to find an answer. Some questions will turn out to be dead ends. You wouldn't have any problem, for instance, finding out more about that ancient pollen to make the account more colorful, but at the time I wrote the book, I could find nothing about Desaulx. All the references I had said that Desaulx proposed the correct explanation for Brownian motion, but no one seemed to know who he was. I'm sure the information is out there, but in the time I had to untangle that particular question, I never got an answer.

That's a lesson in itself. You need to know when to stop. I could have spent days pursuing that little point, but it was only a tiny aside (I was, after all, writing a book about infinity, not Brownian motion), and once it was obvious it would take quite a while to follow up, it was best discarded.

Putting your own opinions alongside the factual content

Facts are essential in any non-fiction piece of work you are going to produce, but fact can be mixed with opinion and interpretation. If you are doing a piece of pure math there is little room for this, but in many subjects – even some aspects of science, and certainly most of the arts – interpretation is crucially important.

You can get plenty of comment and opinion from the web, but one of the big opportunities to turn vanilla information into your own flavor of communication is to include your own opinion and interpretation. Don't just put what happened, but why, or why you *think* it happened. (Make a clear distinction here. Don't state your opinions as fact. That's an easy mistake, but it is always a disaster.)

This is a handy place to bring in five Ws and a H that are constant companions for any good journalist. That's:

* Who?
* What?
* Where?
* When?
* Why? and
* How?

Use these questions both to delve into your facts and to help inspire your interpretation. If all you do is recite facts, you are unlikely to engage the reader's interest. With careful use of opinion – an opportunity for you as an individual to emerge in your writing – you can make all the difference.

Quoting your sources

Unless you are writing fiction, or doing original research, no one expects you to produce all your work off the top of your head. Good academic work is built on the writings of others. Although there is some suspicion that Isaac Newton was being nasty when he commented, "If I have seen further it is by standing on ye shoulders of Giants," because he said this in a letter to a rival, Robert Hooke (Newton was habitually spiteful and may have been referring to the fact that Hooke, who he hated, had a bent back and so was not very tall), there is no doubt that he was right that even genius uses what can be taken from the existing bank of knowledge.

Aside on "standing on the shoulders of Giants"

This quote from Isaac Newton is very famous and is often used to emphasize the fact that creativity isn't usually a solo activity, and that even a small idea can have a big effect when building

> on the contributions of others. But not so many people know that Newton was literally standing on someone else's shoulders in making this remark, because what he wrote was nearly a direct quote from someone else. "Pigmies placed on the shoulders of giants see more than the giants themselves" appeared in Robert Burton's *The Anatomy of Melancholy* more than 50 years before Newton wrote his letter.

There is nothing wrong, then, with getting information from elsewhere. But what is wrong is if you take information from somewhere else and pretend it is all your own original work. It happens all the time. Some authors are particularly bad at admitting how much they rely on the ideas of others. But that doesn't make it right.

If all you have to do for an assignment is write a quick essay, chances are you don't have to worry about this. It will be assumed that you have consulted books and websites and no detail is required. But with a big project, any academic paper or an assignment where you have been asked to provide citations, it is important to keep track of where you got the information from, and to give a clear indication of your sources. (Citations are just details of the sources you used, usually put at the end of the project on a "citations" or "works cited" page.)

There are two reasons for doing this. One is that you make clear just what you got from where. There can be no suggestion of plagiarism, of pretending someone else's work is your own, because you are being open and honest about your sources. The other is that it makes it very helpful for anyone who is going to use your piece of work as a source themselves. They can pick up on the same original material.

If you do need citations, produce them as you go. There is nothing worse than trying to remember at the end of a long project where every bit of information came from (especially as the books you used may well have gone back to the library by then, or the websites forgotten).

Broadly there are three ways to do citations. If they are quite general references, you can simply list the books and websites used at the end of your work. (This is usually called a bibliography.) With more detailed references, you will want to describe which points in your text a particular citation is helpful for. Traditionally these are done with endnotes. A little number appears in your text at the point the reference is being made, and you can look it up at the back of the project to see which citation it refers to.

The only trouble is that these little numbers do rather mess up the page. An alternative is to have end notes that describe how the citation has been used, and the page it comes from. Something like these, from my book *The God Effect*:

Endnotes from *The God Effect*

Page 27 – Shrek's metaphor of ogres being like onions, from the movie *Shrek* (Dreamworks SKG, 2001)

Page 27 – Gribbin's criticism of Herbert for calling the planetary model of the atom wrong comes from Gribbin, John – *Schrödinger's Kittens* (Phoenix 1996)

Page 31 – Momentum is defined as "what [a particle] is doing" in Polkinghorne, J. C. – *The Quantum World* (Penguin, 1990)

Page 34 – Einstein's letter to Born saying he would rather be a cobbler is from Born, Max – *The Born-Einstein Letters* (Macmillan, 1971)

This keeps all the information that links the endnotes to your main text with the notes themselves, so there's no need to have those messy little numbers in your text.

Both types of endnote are made a lot easier by word processor features. In Word, for instance, the numbered type of reference is put in using Reference/Footnote from the Insert menu, then selecting End Notes. (Footnotes are like endnotes, but appear at the bottom of the page where the number is. They are fine to explain something, but messy for citations.) My style of endnotes with no numbers can be set up by putting a bookmark at the point in your text you want the reference to link to (Bookmark from the Insert menu), then using a bookmark cross-reference to put the page number in the end notes (Reference/Cross-reference from the Insert menu). In both cases, by using this approach the reference will stay linked even if the page numbering changes.

You may be asked to provide your citations in a particular form at – the most common is probably MLA formatted, which refers to the US Modern Language Association, which defined a standard way of laying out citations. There is an easy way to produce these, thanks to a website called The Citation Machine – go along to www.citationmachine.net This will ask you for the essential information to produce a citation, then turn it out in MLA format. (It also produces APA format – for some reason the American Psychological Association has its own, different approach.)

If I were doing the Roger Bacon assignment we met in chapter 2, and I was asked to provide an MLA formatted Works Cited page, one of the books that would be included is the one I wrote, *The First Scientist: A Life of Roger Bacon*. If I run Citation Machine on this book, then I get the following citation:

Clegg, Brian. *The First Scientist: A Life of Roger Bacon.* 1st ed. London: Constable & Robinson, 2003.

To be honest, some of this is probably unnecessary. With many books it really doesn't matter which edition you used (about 90 per cent of books never get past the first edition) and the city of publication is a meaningless, out-of-date piece of information in an age of global businesses: it looks positively Victorian. Nowadays you might also want to include the ISBN (see page 48). Even so, if you are asked for MLA format citations, this is what you need to go with the flow and give them what they ask for.

The citation format has also been extended to cope with web pages and other electronic forms, which is just as well if you want to make effective use of the internet. If I want to list something I found on a website it would look something like this:

Clegg, Brian. *Popular Science book review site.* 24 January 2006 <www.popularscience.co.uk>.

While a reference to an email I received in response to a request for help might look something like this:

Smith, Doctor E. E. "Help with essay on Manet locations." E-mail to Brian Clegg. 15 July 2006.

You can do them yourself once you are familiar with the formats, but if in doubt check The Citation Machine.

Proud of what you've done?

Why not share it? If you have really managed to produce something original and interesting that you're proud of, there's no reason why you shouldn't make more of it than just a school or college assignment. See if there's some way to get all or part of it in print. Give the world a treat.

Is there a student newspaper or magazine it would fit in? Is it so original it might be of interest to a commercial magazine? It's entirely possible, particularly if you are dealing with a subject that has specialist interest – and you could even get paid for it. But make sure you understand the way the target magazine works. There's no point submitting a chatty little piece to an academic journal, or sending an essay on Chaucer to a rock music magazine. Also, your writing needs to have a professional feel – if you've any doubt about what's required, have a word with your teacher or tutor.

A more likely way to get your masterpiece in front of the world is if you have access to a website. Get your work published on the school website or your own site. It's also worth checking out the entry for your subject in the Wikipedia online encyclopedia (www.wikipedia. org). If the entry is less than complete, then add some of your material in. The great thing about Wikipedia is that anyone can contribute. (You can also add your own page if there's nothing there at all, but this is ridiculously complicated, so it's best to stick to changing an existing article.)

Making text your own – the essentials

This is probably the most important part of the whole book. Unless you can turn what you've found into your own work, all you are doing is copying. A 4-year-old can copy. You can do something much better (and something that will get you much better grades) – create for yourself.

- Make sure you've made the assignment *yours* – avoid plagiarism (pretending someone else's work is your own), and produce something original with this simple checklist:

- Have you used your own words?
- Have you used multiple sources?
- Have you made the information more readable?
- Have you presented the information in a different way?
- Have you added charts, diagrams, and illustrations?
- Have you pulled together elements of information that didn't previously appear in the same place?
- Have you looked for the questions that a piece of text raises and answered them?
- Have you put your own opinion alongside facts – but made it clear which is which?

- Only use cut and paste for quotes and basic information collection, and collect and modify when time is of the essence. Otherwise either collate and write or, if you know the subject well, write and refine.
- Don't worry if it's too long – you can always edit down. If you have to increase length try using extra information, boxes, and sidebars rather than simply padding.
- Quote your sources and if necessary use proper citations.
- If you are proud of your result, let the world see it – try to get it published on paper or the web.

Chapter 9

Keeping up to date

A lot of the time when you go to the internet to get information it will be for one piece of work. You do the assignment, you use what you've found, then you throw it away. But sometimes there's a subject you need to keep up to date with. Maybe it's a long-term project, a subject you are studying for a qualification, or just something that interests you.

You don't want to have to go out digging for information every time you need more, starting from scratch every time – but luckily the internet isn't one-way traffic. As well as going out to find things, you can ask information to come to you on a regular basis.

RSS rules

The best thing that has happened to the web in a long time, at least if you are looking to keep on top of the news in a subject, is RSS. That stands for Really Simple Syndication, though everyone knows it by the initials. The idea is a simple one. The website publisher has a little file that lists what the most recently updated pages on the site are, with a simple description. If you have a piece of software that can pick up RSS, it will present you with the latest headlines from the site, updated on a regular basis. It's like having your own newspaper, filled with the exact topic you are interested in, updated every few minutes.

> **!**
>
> ## Hot tip – what's this mess?
>
> If you click on an RSS link on a website you may see something like this:
>
> <?xml version="1.0" ?>
> - <rss version="**2.0**">
> - <channel>
>   <title>**Popular Science – book reviews, authors and more**</title>
>   <description>**Our latest reviews of popular science books, features and event listings**</description>
>   <link>**http://www.popularscience.co.uk**</link>
>   <copyright>**2000–2005 Creativity Unleashed Limited**</copyright>
>   <pubDate>**Fri, 9 Dec 2005 16:20:00 GMT**</pubDate>
>   <lastBuildDate>**Fri, 9 Dec 2005 16:20:00 GMT**</lastBuildDate>
> - <item>
>   <title>**Q and A: Cosmic Conundrums and Everyday Mysteries of Science (Surendra Verma)**</title>
>   <description>**Lots of fun and some significant surprises in this selection of answers to the scientific questions we'd all like to ask, but haven't *******</description>
>   <link>**http://www.popularscience.co.uk/reviews/rev241.htm**</link>
>   </item>
>
> Don't worry – you've just looked under the hood at the workings of RSS. This is the file that tells your RSS reader what to display. Just back up and copy the link that you clicked on (in Internet Explorer, right click the RSS box or

> link/control click on a Mac) and select Copy Shortcut; in
> Firefox right click the RSS box or link (control click on
> Mac) and select Copy Link Location, then paste it into your
> RSS reader.

Read all about it

There are three main ways of subscribing to RSS feeds: through a portal, in your web browser or using a news reader.

"Through a portal" sounds worryingly like something from the *Stargate* TV show, but in fact it is just a website like Google, Yahoo, or MSN, that tries to provide for your every need. Each of these services has an option to personalize your home page so that when you go to Google (or whatever) you don't just see the standard search box, but a page with a wide range of additional information. It could be local weather, or a quote of the day . . . or whatever RSS newsfeeds you like.

Google users should click on the Personalized Home link in the top right hand corner. Yahoo users click on My Yahoo, to the right of the main logo. And MSN users click on My MSN just below the search box. In each case you will be asked to register with the service, then will get a basic personalized page with some suggestions of what you can put on it. Each of the items, like an RSS newsfeed, will be placed on panels on your page. Now it gets interesting. You don't need to keep the items you have been given – and you can add others as you like.

With each of the services, you can pick from a list they provide (first you have to click on the Add Content link, usually towards the top left hand corner of the page), or you can tell it about an RSS service that you want to use. Just paste in the RSS address (it will look like a web address, but typically will end in "xml" – for example http://www.popularscience.co.uk/feed.xml). See below for details on finding these and other ways to subscribe to feeds.

In the example below, Google has been personalized with some RSS feeds from various different websites, including the BBC (the content is fictional), ZDNet, Creativity Unleashed, and Popular Science. Clicking the link at the top of each box takes you straight to the relevant home page, while each of the headlines is a link to see the full story.

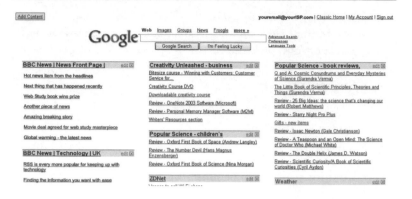

Whichever portal you use, it's possible to rearrange the layout of the page to put your favorite items at the top. Each of the three big portals has a very different presentation, and each has a range of other feeds as well as RSS (for example the "weather" option you can see just at the bottom of the Google page shown here). It's worth sampling all three and deciding which works best for you. There are also other portal pages (for example aol.com) to choose from, including the specialist portal for RSS and blogs, Bloglines (www.bloglines.com).

If you decide to personalize a portal and use it as your view onto the RSS world, you will probably want to make it the page that appears in your browser when you start it up. Make sure you have your personalized page on screen, then select (Internet) Options from the Tools menu and click on Use Current in the home page section.

One word of warning – personalizing a portal with RSS feeds does slow the portal down a little. If you are used to something like Google appearing the instant you click on the browser button, you will find a slight delay. It is short, but can be slightly irritating – decide for yourself whether it's worth it to get your instant news this way.

You may decide you don't want to mess around with your portal – no problem, you can also pick up your RSS feeds via your web browser. If you are using Firefox or Internet Explorer 7 or later, you can use a feed as a live bookmark or favorite, as long as the site you want to get a feed from is set up appropriately (see below for how to do this).

Alternatively, the most sophisticated way to keep track of your RSS feeds is through a newsreader. This is a piece of software that is designed to read the input from RSS feeds and present the results as a kind of electronic newspaper. This sort of facility is increasingly being built into email packages, or you can check out specialist RSS newsreaders such as Newsgator (www.newsgator.com – this also is the site for the leading Mac newsreader, NetNewsWire) and RSS reader (www.rssrcader.com).

Where's the stuff?

It's great being able to see RSS feeds in all these different ways, but how do you get hold of them in the first place? Not all websites provide RSS information, but there are a couple of standard ways of making an RSS feed available.

Look out for a small orange button with the letters RSS:

RSS

on the home page – this should be displayed if the site has an RSS feed. If you click this RSS button, some sites will take you straight to the file that provides the RSS information, in which case you should go back and either right click/control click the RSS button as described above, or drag the orange block into your newsreader. Alternatively, the RSS button may take you to a special page with details of one or more newsfeeds from the site.

Many sites also have "add to" buttons or links, which allow you to add the RSS feed to your portal or newsreader with a single click. There will be a specific button or link for each portal or newsreader the site has information on.

If your preference is to pick up the RSS newsfeed as "live book-marks" (favorites) in your web browser, it can be done if the website has the right information on their page. You can tell whether or not this is the case because the browser will display an "add live book-mark" button. In Firefox it looks like this at the bottom of browser window:

Click on this button and you will see a new folder within your book-marks (favorites) list. Click on that folder and the current headlines open up. You can either navigate to one of them by clicking on it, or use the "open in tabs" option to put each of the headlined pages in a separate tab. Do this with care – there is no limit on the number of entries in an RSS feed, so in principle it could try to open hundreds of tabs, which will take a while and won't do you a lot of good.

If you run your own website, you can also use RSS feeds to incorporate headlines directly into your site. You will need to use an RSS host, which formats the information from the RSS feed and provides it to your site. There are free hosts available, such as www.feeddigest.com

Just a quick letter

RSS feeds are a great way to pick up on the latest headlines, and to dive in and pull out detail, but they aren't very readable. Many websites also provide free newsletters or updates, which combine editorial matter and special offers with news on the latest additions to the site. If you are interested in a subject, it's well worth signing up for a newsletter.

It is only reasonable to be a little wary when doing this. At the very least you are giving a stranger your email address. But you do need to use an email address you check regularly or you won't actually read the newsletter, so there's not a lot of point in subscribing.

A few quick checks make all the difference when signing up. How much information is asked of you? If newsletter signup involves giving your home address or any other personal details, be suspicious, though it's reasonable to be asked which country you are from. Is it made clear what will be done with your email address, and how to remove yourself from the list? All responsible newsletters carry details of how to get off the list in every mailing, as well as on the website. Of course, just because someone says they will behave responsibly doesn't mean they will, but you should expect clear notification. You should also be given some idea of how frequently you will receive an email.

Take the sign-up for the newsletter for the popular science book review site, www.popularscience.co.uk (see below). The website tells you what you are signing up for, and only asks for a name, email address, and country. You are told that your details won't be given to a third party (always reassuring) and that you can remove yourself at any time. This can be done directly from the form you've just used.

This particular newsletter also uses an opt-in method. This means that someone else can't put in your email address and land you with a mailing you don't want. You have to actively confirm that you want the mailing before you receive it. This isn't essential, but it's a good sign of a responsible newsletter.

Newsletter

Want to keep up to date? It's easy to sign up for our free newsletter. Just fill in the form below. It's free, informative and (like the best popular science) always readable. Each newsletter has special book offers, plus a 25% discount on a range of bestselling popular science books if you join before the end of 2005.

Name: [_____]

E-mail: [_____]

Country: [_____]

⦿ Subscribe   ○ Unsubscribe

[Do it!]

How it works: after you complete the form and press the Do it button, an e-mail will be sent to the e-mail address you've given asking you to confirm your subscription.

Your name and details are held securely, and will never be given to any third party. You can remove yourself from the mailing list at any time.

❗ Hot tip – they can be sneaky

On the next page is another signup form for a newsletter. It's not for a real website, but the technique used here is quite common.

You are asked for rather a lot of information, but it doesn't look too bad. After the Go button there are some conditions, but who bothers to read those? And on many screens, you won't see what comes below the conditions – a set of check boxes to choose what sort of contact you would like. Often, boxes that aren't checked mean you won't get contacted. But lurking there in the middle is a box which will result in your getting mail and phone calls if you *don't* check it. Very easy to miss.

Always scroll down below the button that signs you up, just to make sure there aren't any lurking check boxes. Incidentally, some perfectly respectable, big-name companies use this technique. It is legal, even if it is very sneaky. You might still want to sign up to their newsletter, but watch out just what it is you are asking for.

SIGN UP FOR THE NEWSLETTER

Your name:

Your email address:

Your contact number:

Your Address:

Your Postcode:

[Go]

Please complete all fields.

By joining this mailing list you are accepting our terms and conditions. We will hold your details securely and will make sure that they are not used in a way that is contrary to your wishes.

We would like to keep you informed of any new promotions, services or products which we think might interest you. Please keep me informed by: Email ☐

SMS ☐

If you do not want us contact you by post or telephone, please tick this box ☐

We may share your details with carefully selected third parties who may contact you with promotions , services or products by email, post or telephone, is this OK? ☐

Once you have signed up for a newsletter, expect to see an email arrive in your inbox on a regular basis with news – this can be very helpful to keep on top of a subject.

One thing you may need to do. Some mail systems (AOL, for instance) and some anti-spam systems only allow emails into your inbox if they come from a known sender, or the sender has responded to an automated mail. If this applies to your email, make sure you add the source of the email to your "safe" list (sometimes this means putting it in your address book), or you won't receive your newsletter.

What's new, what's good?

One excellent way to keep on top of what's happening in a field you are interested in is to regularly visit a review site. Sites like this will keep your information current on the latest technology, music, or books. Often the site may be linked to a published magazine. So a good way to keep up to date in science, for example, is to visit the New Scientist site at www.newscientist.com, or you can find reviews of new technology at the Ziff Davis site at www.zdnet.com Similarly, the www.popularscience.co.uk website carries reviews of popular science and popular math books, to make it easy to choose which books to read next.

You might not always agree with a review site, but it's a useful way to keep on top of what's happening when you can't otherwise. Many such sites also have newsletters and RSS feeds.

Blog away

There aren't many people who haven't come across blogs (short for web logs) by now. These are effectively public diaries, an opportunity for everyone and anyone to be a columnist and to share their opinions with the world. The blog might be a one-off on an individual's site – take a look at Martian Soil, for instance, at www.martiansoil.com, which is a blog dedicated to the planet Mars – or part of a whole community on a site dedicated to blogging like www.blogger.com

Blogs can be interesting, and if you find a particular blogger whose views are of interest you might like to keep an eye on what they are saying. Often blogs can be collected in a reader using RSS. To use a blog as a reliable source of update information you have to be fairly sure of the blogger's credentials, but there are certainly plenty of people out there worth listening to.

Online exam preparation

One special case of keeping up to date is revising for exams. It's perfectly possible to use the skills you have already gained to pull together the information you need to get through your examinations, but you are unlikely to get the particular combination of information in the compact, easily digestible form that aids revision.

Luckily, there are sites dedicated to helping out with revision. UK students should try **exam revision** in a search engine, or US students **exam preparation**. Just to get you started, UK school students should take a look at the excellent BBC site at www.bbc.co.uk/schools/revision, which includes bite-sized guides and detailed online coursework. Take a look around, but be aware that some of the sites, particularly in the US, do charge.

So what are you waiting for?

You now have the skills to do much more than just copy information from a website. You can break down your assignment into manageable chunks and use good guesswork and intelligent searching to find appropriate websites. You can collect that information, structure it and turn it into something original and interesting. The rest is up to you and your imagination. Have a great time.

Index